CW00791286

© Peter Stewart, 1991
Published by Lochar Publishing Ltd
MOFFAT DG10 9ED

British Library Cataloguing in Publication Data
   Stewart, Peter
   The Football almanac.
   1. Football League   2. Great Britain
   I. Title
   796.334630941

   ISBN 0-948403-77-2

Typeset in 8 on 8½pt Times by Chapterhouse,
Formby L37 3PX
and printed in Scotland by Eagle Colourbooks

Publisher's Note
While every possible care has been taken by the author and
publisher in the compilation and preparation of the
information contained in this publication, because of the
changing nature of the game they can accept no
responsibility for any inaccuracies which may be included
herein.

Contents

Introduction

Have you ever wondered how and when your favourite club was formed?

Want to know their address, telephone number . . . how many honours they've won at home and in Europe . . . their nickname . . . League career . . . top transfer dealings . . . present ground capacity . . . largest ever attendance . . . record victory and defeat . . . managerial changes . . . some former famous players?

Often the answers to these questions can only be found in large, very expensive reference books. Or after painstaking hours wading through various annuals in a library.

Now, thanks to this at-a-glance, easy-to-read-almanac featuring every club in the English and Scottish League all the relevant facts are readily available.

No football fan will want to be without this unique guide . . . at home, or away!

Special Note

Readers are reminded that all 0898 numbers are charged at 34p per minute off peak and 45p per minute at all other times.

The Barclays Football League

ALDERSHOT
Formed: 1926. Turned professional: 1927.
Nickname: Shots.
Address: Recreation Ground, High Street, Aldershot. GU11 1TW.
Telephone: 0252 20211. ClubCall: 0898 121630.
Manager: Brian Talbot.
Ground capacity: 12,000 (10,000 under cover).
Record attendance: 19,138 v Carlisle, FA Cup Fourth Round replay 20th January, 1970.
Record victory: 7-0 v Chelmsford, FA Cup First Round, 28th November, 1931.
Record defeat: 0-9 v Bristol City, Division Three (South), 28th December, 1946.
Record transfer received: £150,000 from Wolves for Tony Lange, July 1989.
Record transfer paid: £54,000 to Portsmouth for Colin Garwood, February 1980.
Honours: None.
Football League record: 1932 elected to Division Three (South); 1958-73 Division Four; 1973-76 Division Three; 1976-87 Division Four; 1987-89 Division Three; 1984 – Division Four.
Managers since the War: Bill McCracken 1937-49; Gordon Clark 1950-55; Harry Evans 1955-59; Dave Smith 1959-71 (general manager from 1967); Tommy McAnearney 1967-68; Jimmy Melia 1968-72; Tommy McAnearney 1972-81; Len Walker 1981-84; Ron Harris (gen. man.) 1984-85; Len Walker 1985-91; Brian Talbot 1991- .
Some famous former players: John Dungworth; Jack Howarth; Peter Scott; Murray Brodie.

Formed in December 1926, the club had no official home ground until the Borough Council purchased 40 acres of land at Aldershot Park a few months later. The Council have leased the Recreation Ground to the club ever since. Their first game against Southend on 27th August, 1927 was watched by a crowd of 3,500. Aldershot lost 2-1.

The club joined the Football League in 1932. In 1954 one

of the BBC's first televised games was staged at the Recreation Ground when Aldershot played The Army to celebrate 100 years of the local Garrison.

A club with no major honours they faced extinction during the 1990 close-season. Only a last minute injection of £250,000 by a local young business man saved them.

ARSENAL

Formed: 1886. Turned professional: 1891.
Nickname: The Gunners
Address: Arsenal Stadium, Highbury, London, N5.
Telephone: 071 226 0303. Recorded information: 071 359 0131. ClubCall: 0898 121170.
Manager: George Graham.
Ground capacity: 57,000.
Record attendance: 73,295 v Sunderland, First Division, 9th March, 1935.
Record victory: 12–0 v Loughborough Town, Second Division, 12th March, 1900.
Record defeat: 0–8 v Loughborough Town, Second Division, 12th December, 1896.
Record transfer received: £1,250,000 from Crystal Palace for Clive Allen, August 1980.
Record transfer paid: £1,300,000 to QPR for David Seaman, May 1990.
Honours: *League Champions*: 1930–31; 1932–33; 1933–34; 1934–35; 1937–38; 1947–48; 1952–53; 1970–71; 1988–89; 1990–91.
FA Cup Winners: 1930; 1936; 1950; 1971; 1979.
League and FA Cup Double: 1970–71.
League Cup (Littlewoods) Winners: 1987.
European Fairs Cup (now UEFA Cup) Winners: 1970.
Football League record: 1893 elected to the Second Division; 1904–13 First Division; 1913–19 Second Division; 1919–First Division.
Managers since the War: George Allison 1934–47; Tom Whittaker 1947–56; Jack Crayston 1956–58; George Swindon 1958–62; Billy Wright 1962–66; Bertie Mee 1966–76; Terry Neill 1976–83; Don Howe 1984–86; George Graham 1986– .
Some famous former players: Cliff Bastin; Joe Mercer; Tommy Lawton; George Armstrong; George Graham;

Malcolm Macdonald; Alan Ball; Pat Jennings; Charlie
George; Charlie Nicholas.

Founded by workers from the Royal Arsenal munitions
factory at Woolwich in 1886. Started playing under the
name Dial Square, the name of one of the workshops. Two
of the players Morris Bates and Fred Beardsley were
formerly with Nottingham Forest. Beardsley wrote to his
old club for help and they responded by supplying Dial
Square with a ball and a full set of red and white shirts. The
club reformed and changed their name to Royal Arsenal
and again in 1891 to Woolwich Arsenal.

Two years later they were elected to the Second Division
and drew their first game 2–2 at home to Newcastle United.

In 1913 the club moved to Highbury Stadium in North
London. From the 1930's onwards the Arsenal became
established as one of the most famous and successful clubs
in the world.

ASTON VILLA

Formed: 1874. Turned professional:
1885.
Nickname: The Villans.
Address: Villa Park, Trinity Road,
Birmingham. B6 6HE.
Telephone: 021 327 6604. ClubCall:
0898 121148.
Manager: Ron Atkinson.
Ground capacity: 41,430.
Record attendance: 76,588 v Derby
Co., FA Cup Sixth Round, 2nd
March, 1946.
Record victory: 13–0 v Wednesday
Old Athletic, FA Cup First Round,
1896.
Record defeat: 1–8 v Blackburn Rovers, FA Cup Third
Round, 16th February, 1889.
Record transfer received: £1,469,000 from Wolves for
Andy Gray, September 1979.
Record transfer paid: £1,500,000 to Millwall for Tony
Cascarino, March 1990.
Honours: *League Champions*: 1893–94; 1895–96;
1896–97; 1898–99; 1899–1900; 1909–10; 1980–81.
Division Two Champions: 1937–38; 1959–60.
Division Three Champions: 1971–72.
FA Cup Winners: 1887; 1895; 1897; 1905; 1913; 1920; 1957.

Double performed: 1896–97.
League Cup winners: 1961; 1975; 1977
European Cup winners: 1981–82.
European Super Cup Winners: 1982–83.
Football League record: 1888 founder member of the
League; 1936–38 Division Two; 1938–59 Division One;
1959–60 Division Two; 1960–67 Division One; 1967–70
Division Two; 1970–72 Division Three; 1972–75 Division
Two; 1975–87 Division One; 1987–88 Division Two;
1988– Division One.
Managers since the War: Alex Massie 1945–50; George
Martin 1950–53; Eric Houghton 1953–58; Joe Mercer
1958–64; Dick Taylor 1965–67; Tommy Cummings
1967–68; Tommy Docherty 1968–70; Vic Crowe 1970–74;
Ron Saunders 1974–82; Tony Barton 1982–84; Graham
Turner 1984–86; Billy McNeill 1986–87; Graham Taylor
1987–90; Dr Josef Venglos 1990–91; Ron Atkinson 1991–.
Some famous former players: Tommy 'Pongo' Waring;
Harry Hampton; Billy Walker; Peter McParland; Derek
Dougan; Charlie Aitken; Andy Gray; Dennis Mortimer;
Chris Nicholl; Jimmy Rimmer; Allan Evans.

Founded in 1974 by members of the Villa Cross Wesleyan
Chapel Cricket Club, in the Aston district of Birmingham,
because they wanted to play football during the winter.

There was a shortage of football clubs in the area at the
time so Villa's very first match was played against a local
rugby club. As a result rugby was played one half and
soccer the other. In 1876 the club moved to Perry Barr and
discovered a hayrick in the middle of their pitch. This had
to be removed before each game and replaced afterwards.

The club became a founder member of the Football
League in 1888 and drew their first game 1-1 away at
Wolverhampton Wanderers.

On Good Friday 1897 Villa played their last game at
Perry Barr, a reserve game against Shrewsbury. The club
moved back to Aston as League and FA Cup double
winners. They were the most powerful club in the country
at the time . . . and have remained one of the most famous
and successful ever since.

BARNET

Formed: 1888. Turned professional: 1965.
Nickname: The Bees
Address: Underhill Stadium, Barnet Lane, Barnet, Herts, EN5 2BE..
Telephone: 081 440 0277.
Manager: Barry Fry.
Ground capacity: 11,120.
Record attendance: 11,026 v Wycombe Wanderers, 1952.
Record victory: 12–0 v Redhill, Athenian League, 1945–46.
Record defeat: 9–2 v Southend, FA Cup 2nd round, 1946–47.
Record transfer received: £350,000 from Wimbledon for Striker Andrew Clarke, 1991.
Record transfer paid: £40,000 for Kenny Lowe from Barrow 1991 and £40,000 for Mark Carter from Runcorn 1991.
Honours: FA Amateur Cup 1945–46; Bob Lord Trophy: 1988–89.
Football League record: 1991 elected to Fourth Division.
Managers in last five years: Barry Fry.
Some famous former players: Jimmy Greaves; Martin Chivers; Robert Codner (Brighton); Nicky Bissett (Brighton); Dave Regis (Notts County); Paul Harding (Notts County); Phil Gridelet (Barnsley).

Barnet Football Club was formed in 1888 and first played in the Olympian League before moving in 1897 to the London League where they won the Division 2 title. In 1906 they amalgamated with Barnet Alston Works and as Barnet Alston FC they won the London League Division One Championship in 1906–07. They moved to their present ground at Underhill in season 1907–08 with the first match being played on 7th September, 1907 against Crystal Palace.

BARNSLEY

Formed: 1887. Turned professional: 1888.

Nickname: The Tykes, Reds or Colliers.

Address: Oakwell Ground, Grove Street, Barnsley.

Telephone: 0226 295353. ClubCall: 0898 121152.

Manager: Mel Machin.

Ground capacity: 30,099 (15,000 under cover).

Record attendance: 40,255 v Stoke City, FA Cup Fifth Round 15th February, 1936.

Record victory: 9–0 v Loughborough Town, Second Division, 28th January, 1899.

Record defeat: 0–9 v Notts County, Second Division, 19th November, 1927.

Record transfer received: £1,400,000 from Nottingham Forest for Carl Tiler, May 1991.

Record transfer paid: £175,000 to Barnet for Phil Gridelet, September 1990.

Honours: *Third Division (North) Champions*: 1933–34; 1938–39; 1954–55.

FA Cup winners: 1912.

Football League record: 1898 elected to the Second Division; 1932–34 Third Division (North); 1934–38 Second Division; 1938–39 Third Division (North); 1946–53 Second Division; 1953–55 Third Division (North); 1955–59 Second Division; 1959–65 Third Division; 1965–68 Fourth Division; 1968–72 Third Division; 1972–79 Fourth Division; 1979–81 Third Division; 1981– Second Division.

Managers since the War: Angus Seed 1937–53; Tim Ward 1953–60; Johnny Steele 1960–71 (continued as General Manager); John McSeveney 1971–72; Johnny Steele (GM) 1972–73; Jim Iley 1973–80; Norman Hunter 1980–84; Bobby Collins 1984–85; Allan Clarke 1985–89; Mel Machin 1989– .

Some famous former players: Cecil McCormack; Ernest Hine; Eddie McMorran; Barry Murphy.

The Rev. Tiverton Preedy, curate of Barnsley St. Peter's founded the club in 1887. They played under that name until 1899, a year after joining the Second Division of the Football League.

Barnsley's first League game was on 1st September, 1898 when they lost 1–0 away at Lincoln City.

The club have always played at Oakwell, but their first pitch was situated behind the present Brewery Stand.

BIRMINGHAM CITY

Formed: 1875. Turned professional: 1885.
Nickname: Blues.
Address: St. Andrews, Birmingham B9 4NH.
Telephone: 021 772 0101/2689.
ClubCall: 0898 121188.
Manager: To be announced.
Ground capacity: 27,689.
Record attendance: 66,844 v Everton, FA Cup Fifth Round, 11th February, 1939.
Record victory: 12–0 v Walsall Town Swifts, Second Division, 17th December, 1892.

Record defeat: 1–9 v Blackburn Rovers, First Division, 5th January, 1895 and v Sheffield Wednesday, First Division 13th December, 1930.
Record transfer received: £975,000 from Nottingham Forest for Trevor Francis, February 1979.
Record transfer paid: £350,000 to Derby County for David Langan, June 1980.
Honours: *Second Division Champions*: 1892–93; 1920–21; 1947–48; 1954–55.
League Cup Winners: 1963; *Leyland Daf Cup Winners*: 1991.
Football League record: First Division: 1894–96; 1901–02; 1903–08; 1921–39; 1948–50; 1955–65; 1972–79; 1980–84; 1985–86; Second Division: 1892–94; 1896–1901; 1902–03; 1908–21; 1946–48; 1950–55; 1965–72; 1979–80; 1984–85; 1986–89; Third Division; 1989– .
Managers since the War: Harry Storer 1945–48; Bob Brocklebank 1949–54; Arthur Turner 1954–58; Pat Beasley 1959–60; Gil Merrick 1960–64; Joe Mallett 1965; Stan Cullis 1965–70; Freddie Goodwin 1970–75; Willie Bell 1975–77; Jim Smith 1978–82; Ron Saunders 1982–86; John Bond 1986–87; Garry Pendrey 1987–89; Dave Mackay 1989–91; Lou Macari 1991– .
Some famous former players: Walter Abbott, Frank Womack, Joe Bradford, Gil Merrick, Malcolm Page, Trevor Francis.

In 1875 several cricket playing members of the local Trinity

Church in the Birmingham district of Bordesley, decided to form a football team to keep them active during the winter months.

They named the club Small Heath Alliance and played on waste land in Arthur Street, close to the present St. Andrews ground. But two years later they moved to Muntz Street.

Small Heath joined the Football League in 1892. Their first match was against Burslem Port Vale and they won 5-1.

The club soon became established in the League and when a crowd of over 29,000 attended a First Division derby against Aston Villa it became apparent that the ground was too small.

The club moved to St. Andrews in 1906 after changing their name to Birmingham, adding the City in 1945.

BLACKBURN ROVERS

Formed: 1875. Turned professional: 1880.
Nickname: Blue and Whites.
Address: Ewood Park, Blackburn. BB2 4JF.
Telephone: 0254 55432.
ClubCall: 0898 121179.
Manager: Donald Mackay.
Ground capacity: 17,819.
Record attendance: 61,783 v Bolton, FA Cup Sixth Round, 2nd March, 1929.
Record victory: 11-0 v Rossendale, FA Cup First Round, 13th October, 1884.
Record defeat: 0-8 v Arsenal, First Division, 25th February, 1933.
Record transfer received: £600,000 from Manchester City for Colin Hendry, November 1989.
Record transfer paid: £750,000 to Barnsley for Steve Agnew, June 1991.

Honours: *First Division Champions*: 1911-12; 1913-14.
Second Division Champions: 1938-39.
Third Division Champions: 1974-75.
FA Cup Winners: 1884; 1885; 1886; 1890; 1891; 1928.
Full Members' Cup Winners: 1986-87.
Football League record: 1888 founder members; 1936-39 Second Division; 1946-47 First Division; 1947-57 Second

Division; 1957–66 First Division; 1966–71 Second Division; 1971–75 Third Division; 1975–79 Second Division; 1979–80 Third Division; 1980– Second Division.
Managers since the War: Bob Crompton 1938–41; Eddie Hapgood 1944–47; Will Scott 1947; Jack Bruton 1947–49; Jackie Bestall 1949–53; Johnny Carey 1953–58; Dally Duncan 1958–60; Jack Marshall 1960–67; Eddie Quigley 1967–70; Johnny Carey 1970–71; Ken Furphy 1971–73; Gordon Lee 1974–75; Jim Smith 1975–78; Jim Iley 1978; John Pickering 1978–79; Howard Kendall 1979–81; Bobby Saxton 1981–86; Don Mackay 1987– .
Some famous former players: Ted Harper; Simon Garner; Bob Crompton; Derek Dougan; Bryan Douglas; Billy Eckersley; Keith Newton; Derek Fazackerley.

The club was founded in 1875, by a group of Old Boys from Blackburn Grammar School.

Became one of the founder members of the Football League in 1888, after winning the FA Cup three years in succession.

Drew their first League match v Accrington Stanley on 15th September, 1888 with an incredible 5–5 scoreline.

Moved to Ewood Park in 1890 after winning the FA Cup for the fifth time.

BLACKPOOL

Formed: 1887. Turned professional: 1887.
Nickname: The Seasiders.
Address: Bloomfield Road Ground, Blackpool FY1 6JJ.
Telephone: 0253 404331. ClubCall: 0898 121648.
Manager: Billy Ayre.
Ground capacity: 12,696.
Record attendance: 38,098 v Wolverhampton Wanderers, First Division, 17th September, 1955.
Record victory: 7–0 v Preston (away), First Division, 1st May, 1948.
Record defeat: 1–10 v Small Heath, Second Division, 2nd March, 1901 and v Huddersfield Town, First Division, 13th December, 1930.
Record transfer received: £330,000 from Leeds United for Paul Hart, March 1978.

Record transfer paid: £116,666 to Sunderland for Jack Ashurst, October 1979.

Honours: *Second Division Champions*: 1929-30.

FA Cup Winners: 1953.

Anglo/Italian Cup Winners: 1971.

Football League record: 1896 elected to the Football League. 1899 failed re-election. 1900 re-elected. 1900-30 Second Division; 1930-33 First Division; 1933-37 Second Division; 1937-67 First Division; 1967-70 Second Division; 1970-71 First Division; 1971-78 Second Division; 1978-81 Third Division; 1981-85 Fourth Division; 1985-90 Third Division; 1990- Fourth Division.

Managers since the War: Joe Smith 1935-58; Ronnie Stuart 1958-67; Stan Mortensen 1967-69; Les Shannon 1969-70; Bob Stokoe 1970-72; Harry Potts 1972-76; Allan Brown 1976-78; Bob Stokoe 1978-79; Stan Ternent 1979-80; Alan Ball 1980-81; Allan Brown 1981-82; Sam Ellis 1982-89; Jimmy Mullen 1989-90; Graham Carr 1990-91; Billy Ayre 1991- .

Some famous former players: Jimmy Hampson; Stan Matthews; Stan Mortensen; George Farm; Ernie Taylor; Jackie Mudie; Jimmy Armfield; Paul Hart; Alan Ball.

The club was born in a bar in the Stanley Arms Hotel during the summer of 1887 when a group of Old Boys of St. John's School decided to form a football team.

Adopting the name of the town, the team played their first season at Raikes Hall Gardens.

They joined the Football League in 1896, losing their first game 3-1 away at Lincoln City.

Three years later, Blackpool amalgamated with South Shore and took over their Bloomfield Road ground where they have played ever since.

BOLTON WANDERERS
Formed: 1874. Turned professional: 1880.
Nickname: The Trotters.
Address: Burnden Park, Bolton. BL3 2QR.
Telephone: 0204 389200. ClubCall: 0898 121164.
Manager: Phil Neal.
Ground capacity: 25,000.
Record attendance: 69,912 v Manchester City, FA Cup Fifth Round, 18th February, 1933.
Record victory: 13–0 v Sheffield United, FA Cup Second Round, 1st February, 1890.

Record defeat: 0–7 v Manchester City, First Division, 21st March, 1936.
Record transfer received: £340,000 from Birmingham City for Neil Whatmore, August 1981.
Record transfer paid: £350,000 to West Bromwich Albion for Len Cantello, May 1979.
Honours: *Second Division Champions*: 1908–09; 1977–78.
Third Division Champions: 1972–73.
FA Cup Winners: 1923; 1926; 1929; 1958.
Sherpa Van Trophy Winners: 1989.
Football League record: 1888 founder members of the League; 1899–1900 Second Division; 1900–03 First Division; 1903–05 Second Division; 1905–08 First Division; 1908–09 Second Division; 1909–10 First Division; 1910–11 Second Division; 1911–33 First Division; 1933–35 Second Division; 1935–64 First Division; 1964–71 Second Division; 1971–73 Third Division; 1973–78 Second Division; 1978–80 First Division; 1980–83 Second Division; 1983–87 Third Division; 1987–88 Fourth Division; 1988– Third Division.
Managers since the War: Walter Rowley 1944–50; Bill Ridding 1951–68; Nat Lofthouse 1968–70; Jimmy McIlroy 1970; Jimmy Meadows 1971; Nat Lofthouse 1971; Jimmy Armfield 1971–74; Ian Greaves 1974–80; Stan Anderson 1980–81; George Mulhall 1981–82; John McGovern 1982–85; Charlie Wright 1985; Phil Neal 1985– .
Some former famous players: Joe Smith; David Jack; Nat Lofthouse; Eddie Hopkinson; Tommy Banks.

The club called themselves the Wanderers because in the

early years they had no particular home ground.

Formed in 1874 by boys of Christ Church Sunday School. Three years later they broke away from the church due to a disagreement with the vicar and changed their name to Bolton Wanderers.

One of the founder members of the Football League in 1888, Bolton lost their first game 6-3 against Derby County.

Bolton have never won the League Championship, but were famous FA Cup fighters in the 1920's, during which time they won the trophy three times.

AFC BOURNEMOUTH

Formed: 1899. Turned professional: 1912.
Nickname: The Cherries.
Address: Dean Court Ground, Bournemouth. BH7 7AF.
Telephone: 0202 395381. ClubCall: 0898 121163.
Manager: Harry Redknapp.
Ground capacity: 11,375.
Record attendance: 28,799 v Manchester United, FA Cup Sixth Round, 2nd March, 1957.
Record victory: 11-0 v Margate, FA Cup First Round, 20th November, 1971.
Record defeat: 0-9 v Lincoln City, Third Division, 18th December, 1982.
Record transfer received: £465,000 from Manchester City for Ian Bishop, August 1989.
Record transfer paid: £210,000 to Gillingham for Gavin Peacock, August 1989.
Honours: *Third Division Champions*: 1986-87.
Associate Members' Cup Winners: 1984.
Football league record: Elected to Third Division (South) 1923. Remained in the Third Division until 1970; 1970-71 Fourth Division; 1971-75 Third Division; 1975-82 Fourth Division; 1982-87 Third Division; 1987-90 Second Division; 1990- Third Division.
Managers since the War: Harry Lowe 1947-50; Jack Bruton 1950-56; Fred Cox 1956-58; Don Welsh 1958-61; Bill McGarry 1961-63; Reg Flewin 1963-65; Fred Cox 1965-70; John Bond 1970-73; Trevor Hartley 1974-78; John Benson 1975-78; Alec Stock 1979-80; David Webb

1980–82; Don Megson 1983; Harry Redknapp 1983– .
Some famous former players: Ted MacDougall; Ron
Eyre; Ray Bumstead; Phil Boyer; Colin Clarke.

The present club were formed in 1890. They called
themselves Boscombe St. Johns and played at King's
Park, situated close to their present home ground at Dean
Court.

The club moved to Castlemain Road, Pokesdown in
1899 as Boscombe FC. Eleven years later they moved back
to Boscombe and Dean Court.

Elected to the Football League Third Division (South) in
1923, losing their first game 3–1 away at Swindon.

Bournemouth added AFC to their name in 1971 in an
effort to get their name at the top of the Football League
alphabetical list. But that has been largely ignored by
statisticians and the media.

They remained a Third Division club for a record
number of years until 1970, when they suffered relegation
to the Fourth.

BRADFORD CITY
Formed: 1903. Turned professional:
1903.
Nickname: The Bantams.
Address: Valley Parade Ground,
Bradford BD8 7DY.
Telephone: 0274 306062.
Manager: John Docherty.
Ground capacity: 14,814.
Record attendance: 39,146 v
Burnley, FA Cup Fourth Round,
11th March, 1911.
Record victory: 11–1 v Rotherham
United, Third Division (North), 25th
August, 1928.
Record defeat: 1–9 v Colchester United, Fourth Division,
30th December, 1961.
Record transfer received: £850,000 from Everton for
Stuart McCall, June 1988.
Record transfer paid: £290,000 to Newcastle United for
Peter Jackson, October 1988.
Honours: *Second Division Champions*: 1907–08.
Third Division Champions: 1984–85.
Third Division (North) Champions: 1928–29.
FA Cup Winners: 1911 (they were the first holders of the
present trophy).

Football League record: 1903 elected to the Second Division; 1908–22 First Division; 1922–27 Second Division; 1927–29 Third Division (North); 1929–37 Second Division; 1937–61 Third Division; 1961–69 Fourth Division; 1969–72 Third Division; 1972–77 Fourth Division; 1977–78 Third Division; 1978–82 Fourth Division; 1982–85 Third Division; 1985–90 Second Division; 1990– Third Division.

Managers since the War: Jack Barker 1946–47; John Milburn 1947–48; David Steele 1948–52; Albert Harris 1952; Ivor Powell 1952–55; Peter Jackson 1955–61; Bob Brocklebank 1961–64; Bill Harris 1965–66; Willie Watson 1966–69; Grenville Hair 1967–68; Jimmy Wheeler 1968–71; Bryan Edwards 1971–75; Bobby Kennedy 1975–78; John Napier 1978; George Mulhall 1978–89; Terry Yorath 1989–90; John Docherty 1990– .

Some famous former players: David Layne; Bobby Campbell; Harry Hampton; Cec Podd; Stuart McCall; Ian Ormondroyd.

Formed from Manningham Rugby Club in 1903 when some of the players decided to turn to soccer in an effort to ease their mounting financial problems.

Named Bradford City, the club members also voted to stay at the Rugby Club's home ground at Valley Parade.

They were immediately elected to the Second Division of the Football League in place of Doncaster Rovers.

The League made the decision to elect Bradford City in an effort to break rugby's popularity in West Yorkshire.

City played their first League game on 1st September, 1903 and lost 2–0 at Grimsby Town.

The club's main stand, built in the summer of 1908, helped to establish Valley Parade as one of the finest grounds in the League with a capacity of 40,000.

That same stand burned down on 11th May, 1985, a tragedy that cost the lives of 56 fans.

BRENTFORD

Formed: 1889. Turned professional: 1899.

Nickname: The Bees.

Address: Griffin Park, Braemar Road, Brentford, Middlesex.TW8 ONT.

Telephone: 081 847 2511. ClubCall: 0898 121108.

Manager: Phil Holder.

Ground capacity: 10,850.

Record attendance: 39,626 v Preston North End, FA Cup Sixth Round, 5th March, 1938.

Record victory: 9–0 v Wrexham, Third Division, 15th October, 1963.

Record defeat: 0–7 v Swansea Town, Third Division (South), 8th November, 1924 and v Walsall, Third Division(South), 19th January, 1957.

Record transfer received: £350,000 from QPR for Andy Sinton, March 1989.

Record transfer paid: £167,000 to Hibernian for Eddie May, July 1989.

Honours: *Second Division Champions*: 1934–35.

Third Division (South) Champions: 1932–33.

Fourth Division Champions: 1962–63.

Football League record: 1920 original member of the Third Division 1921–23 Third Division (South); 1933–35 Second Division; 1935–47 First Division; 1947–54 Second Division; 1954–62 Third Division(South); 1962–63 Fourth Division; 1963–66 Third Division; 1966–72 Fourth Division; 1972–73 Third Division; 1973–78 Fourth Division; 1978– Third Division.

Managers since the War: Harry Curtis 1926–49; Jackie Gibbons 1949–52; Jimmy Blain 1952–53; Tommy Lawton 1953; Bill Dodgin Snr. 1953–57; Malcolm Macdonald 1957–65; Tommy Cavanagh 1965–66; Billy Gray 1966–67; Jimmy Sirrel 1967–69; Frank Blunstone 1969–73; Mike Everitt 1973–75; John Docherty 1975–76; Bill Dodgin Jnr. 1976–80; Fred Callaghan 1980–84; Frank McLintock 1984–87; Steve Perryman 1987–1990; Phil Holder 1990– .

Some famous former players: Jack Holliday; Jim Towers; Dai Hopkins; Ken Coote; Tommy Lawton; Ron Greenwood.

Formed in 1889, they soon became established as one of London's leading amateur clubs, winning many local honours.

The club moved to their present Griffin Park ground in 1904 while still in the Southern League.

Became one of the original members of the Third Division (South) in 1920, losing their first game 3–0 away at Exeter City.

But Brentford won every home game during the 1929–30 season and by 1935 had become a First Division club.

Unfortunately, their record hasn't been so impressive over recent years. There have even been rumours of a merger with neighbouring Queens Park Rangers.

One notable fact that will interest many fans . . . they are the only club in the Football League to have a pub situated on each corner of the stadium.

BRIGHTON AND HOVE ALBION

Formed: 1900. Turned professional: 1900.

Nickname: The Seagulls.

Address: Goldstone Ground, Old Shoreham Road, Hove, Sussex. BN3 7DE.

Telephone: 0273 739535. Seagull Line: 0898 800609.

Manager: Barry Lloyd.

Ground capacity: 18,493.

Record attendance: 36,747 v Fulham, Second Division, 27th December, 1958.

Record victory: 10–1 v Wisbech, FA Cup First Round, 13th November, 1951.

Record defeat: 0–9 v Middlesbrough, Second Division, 23rd August, 1958.

Record transfer received: £900,000 from Liverpool for Mark Lawrenson, August 1981.

Record transfer paid: £500,000 to Manchester United for Andy Ritchie, October 1980.

Honours: *Third Division (South) Champions*: 1957–58. *Fourth Division Champions*: 1964–65.

Football League record: 1920 original member of Third Division; 1921–58 Third Division (South); 1958–62 Second Division; 1962–63 Third Division; 1963–65 Fourth Division; 1965–72 Third Division; 1972–73 Second Division; 1973–77 Third Division; 1977–79 Second Division; 1979–83 First Division; 1983–87 Second Division; 1987–88 Third Division; 1988– Second Division.

Managers since the War: Tommy Cook 1947; Don Welsh

1947-51; Billy Lane 1951-61; George Curtis 1961-63; Archie Macaulay 1963-68; Fred Goodwin 1968-70; Pat Saward 1970-73; Brian Clough 1973-74; Peter Taylor 1974-76; Alan Mullery 1976-81; Mike Bailey 1981-82; Jimmy Melia 1982-83; Chris Cattlin 1983-86; Alan Mullery 1986-87; Barry Lloyd 1987- .
Some famous former players: Tommy Cook; Tug Wilson; Steve Penney; Peter Ward; Mark Lawrenson; Gary Stevens.

In 1900, a professional club called Brighton United were forced to disband due to lack of support.

Their manager John Jackson called the players together and formed a new club called Brighton and Hove Rangers.

Mr.Jackson and his team were so determined to keep the club alive that they helped collect the gate money before kick-off.

A year later the club changed their name again to Brighton and Hove Albion and they played their home games on the Sussex County Cricket Ground.

The club moved to the Goldstone Ground in 1902 to share with Hove FC, who later sold the lease to Albion for £40.

During the early days, sheep were allowed to graze on the Goldstone during the close-season In 1920 the club became a Founder Member of the Third Division. Unfortunately they lost their first game 2-0 away at Southend United.

BRISTOL CITY

Formed: 1894. Turned professional: 1897.
Nickname: The Robins.
Address: Ashton Gate, Bristol. BS3 2EJ.
Telephone: 0272 632812. ClubCall: 0898 121176.
Manager: Jimmy Lumsden.
Ground capacity: 25,271.
Record attendance: 43,335 v Preston North End, FA Cup Fifth Round, 16th February, 1935.
Record victory: 11-0 v Chichester City, FA Cup First Round, 5th November, 1960.
Record defeat: 0-9 v Coventry City, Third Division (South), 28th April, 1934.

Record transfer received: £325,000 from Coventry City for Gary Collier, July 1979.
Record transfer paid: £235,000 to St.Mirren for Tony Fitzpatrick, July 1979.
Honours: *Second Division Champions*: 1905–06.
Third Division (South) Champions: 1922–23; 1926–27; 1954–55.
Welsh Cup Winners: 1934.
AngloScottish Cup Winners: 1977–78.
Freight Rover Trophy Winners: 1985–86.
Football League record: 1901 elected to the Second Division; 1906–11 First Division; 1911–22 Second Division; 1922–23 Third Division (South) 1923–24 Second Division; 1924–27 Third Division (South); 1927–32 Second Division; 1932–55 Third Division (South); 1955–60 Second Division; 1960–65 Third Division; 1965–76 Second Division; 1976–80 First Division; 1980–81 Second Division; 1981–82 Third Division; 1982–84 Fourth Division; 1984–90 Third Division; 1990– Second Division.
Managers since the War: Bob Hewison 1932–49; Bob Wright 1949–50; Pat Beasley 1950–58; Peter Doherty 1958–60; Fred Ford 1960–67; Alan Dicks 1967–80; Bobby Houghton 1980–82; Roy Hodgson 1982; Terry Cooper 1982–88; Joe Jordan 1988–90; Jimmy Lumsden 1990– .
Some famous former players: Billy Wedlock; Don Clark; John Atyeo.

The club was reformed in 1897 when Bristol South End decided to turn professional and apply to join the Southern League.

The new club, Bristol City, persuaded Sam Hollis, a famous name from Woolwich Arsenal to take over as manager. Immediately, the City directors gave Sam £40 to spend on building a new team.

In 1901 City merged with another local club Bedminster, who played at Ashton Gate. They were elected to the Second Division of the Football League the same year, losing their first game 2–0 away at Blackpool.

BRISTOL ROVERS
Formed: 1883. Turned professional: 1897.
Nickname: The Pirates.
Address: Twerton Park, Twerton, Bath.
Club address: 199 Two Mile Hill Road, Kingswood, Bristol. BS15 1AS.
Telephone: 0272 352508. ClubCall: 0898 121631.
Manager: To be announced.
Ground capacity: 9,813.
Record attendance (at Eastville): 38,472 v Preston North End, FA Cup Fourth Round, 30th January, 1960.

Record victory: 7–0 v Brighton and Hove Albion, Third Division (South), 29th November, 1952.
Record defeat: 0–12 v Luton Town, Third Division (South), 13th April, 1936.
Record transfer received: £1,000,000 from Crystal Palace for Nigel Martyn, November 1989.
Record transfer paid: £100,000 to Birmingham City for Stewart Barrowclough, July 1979.
Honours: *Third Division (South) Champions*: 1952–53. *Third Division Champions*: 1989–90.
Football League record: 1920 original member of the Third Division; 1921–53 Third Division (South); 1953–62 Second Division; 1962–74 Third Division; 1974–81 Second Division; 1981–90 Third Division; 1990– Second Division.
Managers since the War: Brough Fletcher 1938–49; Bert Tann 1950–68 (GM until 1972); Fred Ford 1968–69; Bill Dodgin Snr 1969–72; Don Megson 1972–77; Bobby Campbell 1978–79; Harold Jarman 1979–80; Terry Cooper 1980–81; Bobby Gould 1981–83; David Williams 1983–85; Bobby Gould 1985–87; Gerry Francis 1987–91.
Some famous former players: Geoff Bradford; Neil Slatter; Stuart Taylor; Gary Mabbutt.

Known as the Black Arabs when first formed in 1883 because the team wore black shirts. They changed their name to Eastville Rovers a year later; to Bristol Eastville Rovers in 1897 when they turned professional and finally to Bristol Rovers in 1898.

One of the original members of the Third Division in 1920, Rovers lost their first game 2–0 away at Millwall.

In January 1960, Eastville's record crowd of over 38,000 saw Rovers play Preston in an FA Cup-tie. Just

3,576 turned up on 26th April, 1986 to see Rovers' last game on that ground . . . a 1–1 draw against Chesterfield.

A few weeks later the club moved to share Bath City's home ground at Twerton Park. But they hope to build a new 11,000 all-seater stadium at Mangotsfield, Bristol.

BURNLEY

Formed: 1882. Turned professional: 1883.
Nickname: The Clarets.
Address: Turf Moor, Burnley. BB10 4BX.
Telephone: 0282 27777. ClubCall: 0898 121153.
Manager: Frank Casper.
Ground capacity: 25,000.
Record attendance: 54,775 v Huddersfield Town, FA Cup Third Round, 23rd February, 1924.
Record victory: 9–0 v Darwen, First Division, 9th January, 1892; v Crystal Palace, FA Cup Second Round replay, 10th February, 1909; v New Brighton, FA Cup Fourth Round, 26th January, 1957 and v Penrith, FA Cup First Round, 17th November, 1984.
Record defeat: 0–10 v Aston Villa, First Division, 29th August, 1925 and v Sheffield United, First Division, 19th January, 1929.
Record transfer received: £300,000 from Everton for Martin Dobson, August 1974 and from Derby County for Leighton James, November 1975.
Record transfer paid: £165,000 to QPR for Leighton James, September 1978.
Honours: First Division Champions: 1920–21; 1959–60.
Second Division Champions: 1897–98; 1972–73.
Third Division Champions: 1981–82.
FA Cup Winners: 1913–14.
Anglo/Scottish Cup Winners: 1978–79.
Football League record: 1888 original member of the Football League. 1897–98 Second Division; 1898–1900 First Division; 1900–13 Second Division; 1913–30 First Division; 1930–47 Second Division; 1947–71 First Division; 1971–73 Second Division; 1973–76 First Division; 1976–80 Second Division; 1980–82 Third Division; 1982–83 Second Division; 1983–85 Third Division; 1985– Fourth Division.

Managers since the War: Cliff Britton 1945–48; Frank Hill 1948–54; Alan Brown 1954–57; Billy Dougall 1957–58; Harry Potts 1958–70 (GM to 1972); Jimmy Adamson 1970–76; Joe Brown 1976–77; Harry Potts 1977–79; Brian Miller 1979–83; John Bond 1983–84; John Benson 1984–85; Martin Buchan 1985; Tommy Cavanagh 1985–86; Brian Miller 1986–89; Frank Casper 1989– .
Some famous former players: Jerry Dawson; George Beel; Jimmy McIlroy; Adam Blacklaw; Jimmy Adamson; John Connelly; Martin Dobson; Willie Irvine; Brian Flynn.

In May 1882 at the Bull Hotel, members of the Calder Vale based Burnley Rovers Rugby Club arranged a meeting to form a football team.

The club moved to Turf Moor shortly after dropping the name Rovers. As the name implies, the ground was originally a patch of turf surrounded by moor.

Turf Moor is believed to have been the first football stadium visited by Royalty when Queen Victoria's son Prince Albert saw Burnley play Bolton in October 1886.

They also played in the first FA Cup Final to be watched by a reigning monarch when King George V saw them beat Liverpool 1–0 at Crystal Palace.

Two years later they became one of the founder members of the Football League, losing their first game 5–2 away at Preston North End.

Although Burnley are no longer the proud First Division force they once were, Turf Moor remains one of the finest stadiums in the country.

BURY
Formed: 1885. Turned professional: 1885.
Nickname: The Shakers.
Address: Gigg Lane, Bury, BL9 9HR.
Telephone: 061 764 48812. ClubCall: 0898 121197.
Manager: Mike Walsh.
Ground capacity: 8,000.
Record attendance: 35,000 v Bolton Wanderers, FA Cup Third Round, 9th January, 1960.
Record victory: 12–1 v Stockton, FA Cup First Round replay, 2nd February, 1897.
Record defeat: 0–10 v Blackburn Rovers, FA Cup

Preliminary Round, 1st October, 1887 and v West Ham United, Milk Cup Second Round second-leg, 25th October, 1983.

Record transfer received: £150,000 from Chesterfield for Danny Wilson, July 1980 and from Everton for Neville Southall, July 1981.

Record transfer paid: £95,000 to Swansea City for Alan Knill, August 1989.

Honours: *Second Division Champions*: 1894–95. *Third Division Champions*: 1960–61. *FA Cup Winners*: 1900; 1903.

Football League record: 1894 elected to the Second Division; 1895–1912 First Division; 1912–24 Second Division; 1924–29 First Division; 1929–57 Second Division; 1957–61 Third Division; 1961–67 Second Division; 1967–68 Third Division; 1968–69 Second Division; 1969–71 Third Division; 1971–74 Fourth Division; 1974–80 Third Division; 1980–85 Fourth Division; 1985– Third Division.

Managers since the War: Norman Bullock 1945–49; John McNeil 1950–53; Dave Russell 1953–61; Bob Stokoe 1961–65; Bert Head 1965–66; Les Shannon 1966–69; Jack Marshall 1969; Les Hart 1970; Tommy McAnearney 1970–72; Alan Brown 1972–73; Bobby Smith 1973–77; Bob Stokoe 1977–78; David Hatton 1978–79; Dave Connor 1979–80; Jim Iley 1980–84; Martin Dobson 1984–89; Sam Ellis 1989–91; Mike Walsh 1991– .

Some famous former players: Norman Bullock; Bill Gorman; Craig Madden; Neville Southall.

Officially formed in April 1885, when members of the Bury Wesleyans and Unitarians football clubs met at the Old White Horse Hotel and decided to amalgamate.

The new club, Bury, acquired a piece of land from the Earl of Derby and built Gigg Lane, which has remained their home ground ever since.

Bury joined the Football League in 1894, winning their first game 4–2 against Manchester City at Gigg Lane.

CAMBRIDGE UNITED

Formed: 1919. Turned professional: 1946.

Nickname: United.

Address: Abbey Stadium, Newmarket Road, Cambridge.

Telephone: 0223 241237. ClubCall: 0898 121141.

Manager: John Beck.

Ground capacity: 10,218.

Record attendance: 14,000 v Chelsea, 1st May, 1970, a friendly to inaugurate the club's new floodlights.

Record victory: 6–0 v Darlington, Fourth Division, 18th September, 1971.

Record defeat: 0–6 v Aldershot, Third Division, 13th April, 1974; v Darlington, Fourth Division, 28th September, 1974 and v Chelsea, Second Division, 15th January, 1983.

Record transfer received: £350,000 from Derby County for Alan Biley, January 1980.

Record transfer paid: £140,000 to Northampton Town for George Reilly, November 1979.

Honours: *Fourth Division Champions*: 1976–77; *Third Division Champions*: 1990–1.

Football League record: 1970 elected to the Fourth Division; 1973–74 Third Division; 1974–77 Fourth Division; 1977–78 Second Division; 1978–84 Second Division; 1984–85 Third Division; 1985–90 Fourth Division; 1990–91 Third Division; 1991– Second Division.

Managers since the War: Bill Whittaker 1949–55; Gerald Williams 1955; Bert Johnson 1955–59; Bill Craig 1959–60; Alan Moore 1960–63; Roy Kirk 1964–66; Bill Leivers 1967–74; Ron Atkinson 1974–78; John Docherty 1978–83; John Ryan 1984–85; Ken Shellito 1985; Chris Turner 1985–90; John Beck 1990– .

Some former famous players: Tom Finney; Steve Spriggs; Alan Biley; David Crown.

Formed in 1919 the club was named Abbey United because their ground was situated in the Abbey district of Cambridge.

The club didn't become Cambridge United until 1949 when they turned professional, operating in the local non-Leagues.

United graduated to the more powerful Southern League in 1958, but were looking to reach Football League status.

They achieved that in 1970 when the club was elected to the Fourth Division to replace Bradford Park Avenue.

United's first League game, against Lincoln City at the Abbey Stadium on 15th August, 1970 ended in a 1-1 draw.

CARDIFF CITY

Formed: 1899. Turned professional: 1910.

Nickname: The Bluebirds.

Address: Ninian Park, Cardiff. CF1 8SX.

Telephone: 0222 398636. ClubCall: 0898 121171.

Manager: To be announced.

Ground capacity: 19,300.

Record attendance: 61,566, Wales v England, 14th October, 1961.

Club record: 57,893 v Arsenal, First Division, 22nd April, 1953.

Record victory: 8-0 v Enfield, FA Cup First Round, 28th November, 1931.

Record defeat: 2-11 v Sheffield United, First Division, 1st January, 1926.

Record transfer received: £215,000 from Portsmouth for Jimmy Gilligan, October 1989.

Record transfer paid: £180,000 to San Jose Earthquakes for Godfrey Ingram, September 1982.

Honours: *Third Division (South) Champions; 1946-47.*

FA Cup Winners: 1926-27 (only time the FA Cup has been won by a club outside England).

Welsh Cup Winners: 20 times.

Football League record: 1920 elected to the Second Division; 1921-29 First Division; 1929-31 Second Division; 1931-47 Third Division (South); 1947-52 Second Division; 1952-57 First Division; 1957-60 Second Division; 1960-62 First Division; 1962-75 Second Division; 1975-76 Third Division; 1976-82 Second Division; 1982-83 Third Division; 1983-85 Second Division; 1985-86 Third Division; 1986-88 Fourth Division; 1988-90 Third Division; 1990- Fourth Division.

Managers since the War: Billy McCandless 1946-48; Cyril Spiers 1948-54; Trevor Morris 1954-58; Bill Jones 1958-62; George Swindon 1962-64; Jimmy Scoular 1964-73; Frank O'Farrell 1973-74; Jimmy Andrews 1974-78; Richie Morgan 1978-82; Len Ashurst 1982-84; Jimmy Goodfellow 1984; Alan Durban 1984-86; Frank Burrows 1986-89; Len Ashurst 1990-91.

Some former famous players: Stan Richards; Len Davies; Alf Sherwood; Phil Dwyer; Trevor Ford; Ivor Allchurch; John Charles; John Toshack.

In 1899 members of the Riverside Cricket Club formed a football team and played on a make-shift pitch at Roath.

Six years later, they moved to Sophia Gardens, a public park on the banks of the River Taff which is now the headquarters of the Glamorgan County Cricket Club.

In 1905, Cardiff became a City and Riverside tried to adopt the name. But they had to wait until 1908 before the Welsh FA granted the club permission to call themselves Cardiff City.

Two years later, on 1st September, 1910, City played the current League Champions Aston Villa to officially open their new ground at Ninian Park. A crowd of over 7,000 saw Cardiff narrowly lose 2–1.

In 1920 the club were elected to the Second Division. They won their first League game, 5–2 away at Stockport County.

CARLISLE UNITED

Formed: 1903. Turned professional: 1921.

Nickname: The Cumbrians or The Blues.

Address: Brunton Park, Carlisle. CA1 1LL.

Telephone: 0228 26237. ClubCall: 0898 121632.

Manager: Aidan McCaffery.

Ground capacity: 18,506.

Record attendance: 27,500 v Birmingham City, FA Cup Third Round, 5th January, 1957 and v Middlesbrough, FA Cup Fifth Round, 7th February, 1970.

Record victory: 8–0 v Hartlepools United, Third Division (North), 1st September, 1928.

Record defeat: 1–11 v Hull City, Third Division (North), 14th January, 1939.

Record transfer received: £275,000 from Vancouver Whitecaps for Peter Beardsley, April 1981.

Record transfer paid: £120,000 to York City for Gordon Staniforth, October 1979.

Honours: *Third Division Champions*: 1964–65.

Football League record: 1928 elected to the Third Division

(North); 1958–62 Fourth Division; 1962–63 Third
Division; 1963–64 Fourth Division; 1964–65 Third
Division; 1965–74 Second Division; 1974–75 First
Division; 1975–77 Second Division; 1977–82 Third
Division; 1982–86 Second Division; 1986–87 Third
Division; 1987– Fourth Division.

Managers since the War: Ivor Broadis 1946–49; Bill
Shankly 1949–51; Fred Emery 1951–58; Andy Beattie
1958–60; Ivor Powell 1960–63; Alan Ashman 1963–67;
Tim Ward 1967–68; Bob Stokoe 1968–70; Ian MacFarlane
1970–72; Alan Ashman 1972–75; Dick Young 1975–76;
Bobby Moncur 1976–80; Martin Harvey 1980; Bob Stokoe
1980–85; Bryan 'Pop' Robson 1985; Bob Stokoe 1985–86;
Harry Gregg 1986–87; Cliff Middlemass 1987–1991; Aidan
McCaffery 1991– .

Some former famous players: Jimmy McConnell; Ivor
Broadis; Eric Walsh; Alan Ross; Peter Beardsley.

Formed in 1903 when Shaddongate United and Carlisle
Red Rose amalgamated.

The club moved to their present Brunton Park ground in
1909, but it was not developed to any extent until they were
elected to the Third Division (North) in 1928.

Carlisle won their first League match, 3–2 away at
Accrington Stanley.

CHARLTON ATHLETIC

Formed: 1905. Turned professional:
1920.
Nickname: The Haddicks; The
Robins or The Valiants.
Address: Selhurst Park, London
SE25 6PH.
Telephone: 081 771 6321. ClubCall:
0898 121146.
Manager: To be announced.
Ground capacity: 31,000.
*Record attendance (at The
Valley)*: 75,031 v Aston Villa, FA
Cup Fifth Round, 12th February,
1938.

Record victory: 8–1 v Middlesbrough, First Division, 12th
September, 1953.
Record defeat: 1–11 v Aston Villa, Second Division, 14th
November, 1959.
Record transfer received: £700,000 from Sheffield
Wednesday for Paul Williams, August 1990.
Record transfer paid: £600,000 to Chelsea for Joe

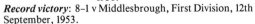

McLaughlin, August 1989.

Honours: *Third Division (South) Champions*: 1928–29; 1934–35.

FA Cup Winners: 1947.

Football League record: 1921 elected to Third Division (South); 1929–33 Second Division; 1933–35 Third Division (South); 1935–36 Second Division; 1936–57 First Division; 1957–72 Second Division; 1972–75 Third Division; 1975–80 Second Division; 1980–81 Third Division; 1981–86 Second Division; 1986–90 First Division; 1990– Second Division.

Managers since the War: Jimmy Seed 1933–56; Jimmy Trotter 1956–61; Frank Hill 1961–65; Bob Stokoe 1965–67; Eddie Firmani 1967–70; Theo Foley 1970–74; Andy Nelson 1974–79; Mike Bailey 1979–81; Alan Mullery 1981–82; Ken Craggs 1982; Lennie Lawrence 1982– .

Some former famous players: Ralph Allen; Stuart Leary; Sam Bartram; John Hewie; Derek Ufton; Eddie Firmani; Mike Bailey; Derek Hales; Mike Flanagan; Allan Simonsen.

When Charlton were formed in 1905, they were just one of several fine amateur clubs in an area more famous for rugby.

By 1920, they had played on seven different home grounds before taking over a well-situated old chalk pitch in Charlton village.

Hundreds of supporters helped dig out the natural bowl to form the shape of a football ground that was aptly named The Valley.

The ground was still without a grandstand when Charlton joined the newly formed Third Division (South) a year later. The club won their first League match, 1–0 away at Exeter.

Sadly The Valley deteriorated over the years until it was forced to close in May 1985.

Several clubs, including Arsenal, considered sharing their ground with Charlton before an arrangement was agreed with Crystal Palace. But Charlton never settled at Selhurst Park and at the end of the 1990–91 season announced their return to a redeveloped Valley.

CHELSEA
Formed: 1905. Turned professional: 1905.
Nickname: The Blues.
Address: Stamford Bridge, Fulham Road, London SW6.
Telephone: 071 3855545. ClubCall: 0898 121159. Ken Bates Hotline: 0898 664666.
Manager: Ian Porterfield.
Ground capacity: 43,900 (21,500 under cover).
Record attendance: 82,905 v Arsenal, First Division, 30th September, 1935.
Record victory: 13–0 v Jeunesse Hautcharage, European Cup-Winners' Cup First Round (second leg), 29th September, 1971.
Record defeat: 1–8 v Wolverhampton Wanderers, First Division, 26th September, 1953.
Record transfer received: £925,000 from Everton for Pat Nevin, July 1988.
Record transfer paid: £1,600,000 to Wimbledon for Dennis Wise, May 1990.
Honours: League Champions: 1954–55.
Second Division Champions: 1983–84; 1988–89.
FA Cup Winners: 1970.
Football League Cup Winners: 1964–65.
Full Members Cup Winners: 1985–86.
Zenith Data Cup Winners: 1989–90.
European Cup Winners' Cup Winners: 1970–71.
Football League record: 1905 elected to the Second Division; 1907–10 First Division; 1910–12 Second Division; 1912–24 First Division; 1924–30 Second Division; 1930–62 First Division; 1962–63 Second Division; 1963–75 First Division; 1975–77 Second Division; 1977–79 First Division; 1979–84 Second Division; 1985–88 First Division; 1988–89 Second Division; 1989– First Division.
Managers since the War: Billy Birrell 1939–52; Ted Drake 1952–61; Tommy Docherty 1962–67; Dave Sexton 1967–74; Ron Suart 1974–75; Eddie McCreadie 1975–77; Ken Shellito 1977–78; Danny Blanchflower 1978–79; Geoff Hurst 1979–81; John Neal 1981–85; John Hollins 1985–88; Bobby Campbell 1988–91; Ian Porterfield 1991–.
Some former famous players: Fatty Foulkes; Tommy Docherty; Jimmy Greaves; Peter Bonetti; Ron Harris; John Hollins; Peter Osgood; Alan Hudson; Bobby Tambling; Ray Wilkins.

In 1904, after an eight year battle for ownership two brothers, H. A. and J. T. Mears, acquired Stamford Bridge, the home of the London Athletics Club. Despite a lucrative offer from the Great Western Railway, who wanted the site for a coal dumping yard, the Mears brothers decided to go ahead with their ambitious plan to form a football club and turn Stamford Bridge into the biggest and finest soccer stadium in the country.

A year later Chelsea FC was formed after nearby Fulham FC had rejected an offer from the Mears brothers to rent Stamford Bridge.

When Chelsea's application to join the Southern League was turned down, they gained immediate entry to the Second Division of the Football League.

Chelsea lost their first League game, 1–0 away at Stockport County. But a week later, they beat Hull City 5–1 in their first League match at The Bridge.

Today there is a great deal of speculation as to whether Chelsea will remain at Stamford Bridge, and develop the stadium into one of the most modern in the League. So, the Mears brothers' dream could yet come true.

CHESTER CITY

Formed: 1884. Turned professional: 1902.
Nickname: The Blues.
Address: The Stadium, Sealand Road, Chester. CH1 4LW.
Telephone: 0244 371376. ClubCall: 0898 121633.
Manager: Harry McNally.
Ground capacity: 10,000.
Record attendance: 20,500 v Chelsea, FA Cup Third Round replay, 16th January, 1952.
Record victory: 12–0 v York City, Third Division (North), 1st February, 1936.
Record defeat: 2–11 v Oldham Athletic, Third Division (North), 19th January, 1952.
Record transfer received: £300,000 from Liverpool for Ian Rush, May 1980.
Record transfer paid: £45,000 to Carlisle United for Steve Ludlam, May 1980.
Honours: Welsh Cup Winners: 1908; 1933; 1947.
Debenhams Cup Winners: 1977.

Football League record: 1931 elected to the Third Division (North); 1958–75 Fourth Division; 1975–82 Third Division; 1982–86 Fourth Division; 1986– Third Division.
Managers since the War: Frank Brown 1938–53; Louis Page 1953–56; John Harris 1956–59; Stan Pearson 1959–61; Bill Lambton 1962–63; Peter Hauser 1963–68; Ken Roberts 1968–76; Alan Dakes 1976–82; Cliff Sear 1982; John Sainty 1982–83; John McGrath 1984; Harry McNally 1985– .
Some former famous players: Dick Yates; Gary Talbot; Bill Lewis; Ray Gill; Ian Rush.

The present club was formed in 1894, when King's School Old Boys amalgamated with Chester Rovers.

Chester had three home grounds before moving to their present Sealand Road in 1906.

They joined the Third Division (North) in 1931 and held Wrexham to a 1–1 draw in their first game.

The same year, the club became one of the first in the Football League to install a public address system at their ground.

CHESTERFIELD

Formed: 1866. Turned professional: 1891.
Nickname: The Blues or The Spireites.
Address: Recreation Ground, Chesterfield. S40 4SX.
Telephone: 0246 209765. ClubCall: 0898 121573.
Manager: Chris McMenemy.
Ground capacity: 11,638.
Record attendance: 30,968 v Newcastle United, Second Division, 2nd April, 1939.
Record victory: 10–0 v Glossop, Second Division, 17th January, 1903.
Record defeat: 0–10 v Gillingham, Third Division, 5th September, 1987.
Record transfer received: £200,000 from Wolverhampton Wanderers for Alan Birch, August 1981.
Record transfer paid: £150,000 to Carlisle United for Phil Bonnyman, March 1980.
Honours: *Third Division (North) Champions*: 1930–31; 1935–36.

Fourth Division Champions: 1969–70; 1984–85.
Anglo/Scottish Cup Winners: 1980–81.
Football League record: 1899 elected to the Second
Division; 1909 failed re-election; 1921–31 Third Division
(North); 1931–33 Second Division; 1933–36 Third Division
(North); 1936–51 Second Division; 1951–58 Third Division
(North); 1958–61 Third Division; 1961–70 Fourth Division;
1970–83 Third Division; 1983–85 Fourth Division; 1985–89
Third Division; 1989– Fourth Division.
Managers since the War: Bob Brocklebank 1945–48;
Bobby Marshall 1948–52; Ted Davison 1952–58; Duggie
Livingstone 1958–62; Tony McShane 1962–67; Jimmy
McGuigan 1967–73; Joe Shaw 1973–76; Arthur Cox
1976–80; Frank Barlow 1980–83; John Duncan 1983–87;
Kevin Randall 1987–88; Paul Hart 1988–91; Chris
McMenemy 1991– .
Some former famous players: Jimmy Cookson; Ernie
Moss; Walter McMillen; Dave Blakey; Gordon Banks.

The fourth oldest club in the Football League, with origins
dating back to 1866.

Chesterfield played at Spital, near the town centre,
before moving to the Recreation Ground in 1884.

The club was elected to the Second Division in 1899,
losing their first game 5–1 away at Sheffield Wednesday.

The club was the last in the Football League to install
floodlights. They were finally switched on by Sir Stanley
Rous for a friendly v Sheffield Wednesday in October
1967.

COVENTRY CITY
Formed: 1883. Turned professional:
1893.
Nickname: Sky Blues.
Address: Highfield Road Stadium,
King Richard Street, Coventry
CV2 4FW.
Telephone: 0203 257171. ClubCall:
0898 121166.
Manager: Terry Butcher.
Ground capacity: 26,218.
Record attendance: 51,455 v
Wolverhampton Wanderers, Second
Division, 29th April, 1967.
Record victory: 9–0 v Bristol City,
Third Division (South), 28th April, 1934.

Record defeat: 2–10 v Norwich City, Third Division
(South), 15th March, 1930.
Record transfer received: £1,250,000 from Nottingham
Forest for Ian Wallace, July 1980.
Record transfer paid: £900,000 to Dundee United for
Kevin Gallacher, January 1990.
Honours: *Second Division Champions*: 1966–67.
Third Division Champions: 1963–64.
Third Division (South) Champions: 1935–36.
FA Cup Winners: 1986–87.
Football League record: 1919 elected to the Second
Division; 1925–26 Third Division (North); 1926–36 Third
Division (South); 1936–52 Second Division; 1952–58 Third
Division (South); 1958–59 Fourth Division; 1959–64 Third
Division; 1964–67 Second Division; 1967– First Division.
Managers since the War: Dick Bayliss 1945–47; Billy Frith
1947–48; Harry Storer 1948–53; Jack Fairbrother 1953–54;
Charlie Elliott 1954–55; Jesse Carver 1955–56; Harry
Warren 1956–57; Billy Frith 1957–61; Jimmy Hill 1961–67;
Noel Cantwell 1967–72; Bob Dennison 1972–81; Dave
Sexton 1981–83; Bobby Gould 1983–84; Don Mackay
1985–86; George Curtis 1985–86; John Sillett 1987–90;
Terry Butcher 1990– .
Some former famous players: Clarrie Bourton; Dave
Clements; George Curtis; Colin Stein.

Formed by workers at the Singers cycle factory in 1883.

By 1908 Singers FC had changed their name to Coventry
City, moved to Highfield Road and were playing in the
Southern League.

The club was elected to the Second Division 11 years
later, winning their first League game 3–2 away at
Rotherham.

A revolution named Jimmy Hill hit the club like a
typhoon in the early Sixties when he took over as manager.

Within ten years Hill had helped transform the club on a
Sky Blue theme. Among the many pioneering ideas
launched during Jimmy Hill's reign was to turn Highfield
Road into the first all-seater stadium in the Football
League.

CREWE ALEXANDRA
Formed: 1877. Turned professional: 1893.
Nickname: The Railwaymen.
Address: Football Ground, Gresty Road, Crewe.
Telephone: 0270 213014.
ClubCall: 0898 121647.
Manager: Dario Gradi.
Ground capacity: 7,200.
Record attendance: 20,000 v Tottenham Hotspur, FA Cup Fourth Road, 30th January, 1960.
Record victory: 8–0 v Rotherham United, Third Division (North), 1st October, 1932.
Record defeat: 2–13 v Tottenham Hotspur, FA Cup Fourth Round replay, 3rd February, 1960.
Record transfer received: £300,000 from Coventry City for Paul Edwards, March 1990.
Record transfer paid: £80,000 to Barnsley for Darren Foreman, March 1990.
Honours: None.
Football League record: 1892 original member of Second Division; 1896 failed re-election; 1921 re-entered Third Division (North); 1958–63 Fourth Division; 1963–64 Third Division; 1964–68 Fourth Division; 1968–69 Third Division; 1969–89 Fourth Division; 1989–91 Third Division; 1991– Fourth Division.
Managers since the War: Frank Hill 1944–48; Arthur Turner 1948–51; Harry Catterick 1951–53; Ralph Ward 1953–55; Maurice Lindlay 1955–58; Harry Ware 1958–60; Jimmy McGuigan 1960–64; Ernie Tagg 1964–71; Dennis Viollet 1971; Jimmy Melia 1972–73; Ernie Tagg 1974; Harry Gregg 1975–78; Warwick Rimmer 1978–79; Tony Waddington 1979–81; Arfon Griffiths 1981–82; Peter Morris 1982–83; Dario Gradi 1983– .
Some former famous players: Terry Harkin; Bert Swindells; Bill Lewis; Tommy Lowry; David Platt; Geoff Thomas.

The club played rugby and cricket before introducing soccer in 1877. The name Alexandra is taken from the pub where the club members held their meetings.

Crewe became one of the original members of the Second Division in 1892. They didn't make an impressive start to their League career, losing 7–1 away at Burton Swifts.

CRYSTAL PALACE
Formed: 1905. Turned professional: 1905.
Nickname: The Eagles.
Address: Selhurst Park, London SE25 6PU.
Telephone: 081 653 4462. ClubCall: 0898 121145.
Manager: Steve Coppell.
Ground capacity: 31,439.
Record attendance: 51,482 v Burnley, Second Division, 11th May,1979.
Record victory: 9–0 v Barrow, Fourth Division, 10th October, 1959.
Record defeat: 0–9 v Liverpool, First Division, 12th September, 1989.
Record transfer received: £800,000 from Arsenal for Kenny Sansom, August 1980.
Record transfer paid: £1,000,000 to Bristol Rovers for Nigel Martyn, November 1989.
Honours: *Second Division Champions*: 1978–79.
Third Division (South) Champions: 1920–21.
Zenith Data Systems Cup Winners: 1990–91.
Football League record: 1920 original members of the Third Division; 1921–25 Second Division; 1925–58 Third Division (South); 1958–61 Fourth Division; 1961–64 Third Division; 1964–69 Second Division; 1969–73 First Division; 1973–74 Second Division; 1974–77 Third Division; 1977–79 Second Division; 1979–81 First Division; 1981–89 Second Division; 1989– First Division.
Managers since the War: Jack Butler 1947–49; Ronnie Rooke 1949–50; Charlie Slade and Fred Dawes (joint managers) 1950–51; Laurie Scott 1951–54; Cyril Spiers 1954–58; George Smith 1958–60; Arthur Rowe 1960–63; Dick Graham 1963–66; Bert Head 1966–73; Malcolm Allison 1973–76; Terry Venables 1976–80; Ernie Walley 1980; Malcolm Allison 1980–81; Dario Gradi 1981; Steve Kember 1981–82; Alan Mullery 1982–84; Dave Bassett 1984; Steve Coppell 1984– .
Some former famous players: Peter Simpson; Paddy Mulligan; Ian Walsh; Peter Nicholas; Vic Rouse; Jim Cannon; Gerry Francis; Clive Allen; Mike Flanagan; Kenny Sansom; Terry Venables.

Formed in 1861 by workers of the company that owned the great Crystal Palace Exhibition building.

The players wanted to turn professional in 1904, but the

Football Association rejected their application because they didn't approve of the Cup Final's hosts having their own club.

A new company was formed in 1915. Four years later Crystal Palace FC moved from the old Cup Final venue to The Nest, situated in the Selhurst district of South London.

Palace kicked off their Football League career in August 1920, losing 2-1 away at Merthyr Tydfil.

The club bought Selhurst Park for £2,570 in January 1922. The ground needed a great deal of redevelopment, including the removal of two giant chimney stacks from where the playing pitch is now sited.

DARLINGTON

Formed: 1883. Turned professional: 1908.
Nickname: The Quakers.
Address: Feethams Ground, Darlington.
Telephone: 0325 465097. ClubCall: 0898 121149.
Manager: Frank Gray.
Ground capacity: 10,932.
Record attendance: 21,023 v Middlesbrough, Third Division, 8th November, 1986.
Record victory: 9-2 v Lincoln City, Third Division (North), 7th January, 1928.
Record defeat: 0-10 v Doncaster Rovers, Fourth Division, 25th January, 1964.
Record transfer received: £150,000 from Barnsley for David Currie, February 1988.
Record transfer paid: £40,000 to Hartlepool United for Andy Toman, July 1989.
Honours: *Third Division (North) Champions*: 1924-25; *Fourth Division Champions*: 1990-91.
Football League record: 1921 original member of Third Division (North); 1925-27 Second Division; 1927-58 Third Division (North); 1958-66 Fourth Division; 1966-67 Third Division; 1967-85 Fourth Division; 1985-87 Third Division; 1987-89 Fourth Division; 1989-90 GM Vauxhall Conference; 1990-91 Fourth Division; 1991- Third Division.
Managers since the War: Bill Forrest 1946-50; George Irwin 1950-52; Bob Gurney 1952-57; Dick Duckworth 1957-60; Eddie Carr 1960-64; Lol Morgan 1964-66; Jimmy Greenhalgh 1966-68; Ray Yeoman 1968-70; Len

Richley 1970–71; Frank Brennan 1971; Ken Hale 1971–72; Allan Jones 1972; Ralph Brand 1972–73; Dick Connor 1973–74; Billy Horner 1974–76; Peter Madden 1976–78; Len Walker 1978–79; Billy Elliott 1979–83; Cyril Knowles 1983–87; Dave Booth 1987–89; Brian Little 1989–91; Frank Gray 1991–

Some former famous players: David Brown; Alan Walsh; Ron Greener; David Currie.

The club began in 1883, but had an early history of financial problems until 1917, when they merged with Darlington Forge Albion, a successful local side.

One of the founder members of the Third Division (North) in 1921, Darlington defeated Halifax Town 2–0 in their first League game in August that year.

The club have experienced an undistingushed career since then, including a season in the GM Vauxhall Conference.

DERBY COUNTY

Formed: 1884. Turned professional: 1884.
Nickname: The Rams.
Address: Baseball Ground, Shaftesbury Crescent, Derby. DE3 8NB.
Telephone: 0332 40105. ClubCall: 0898 121187.
Manager: Arthur Cox.
Ground capacity: 24,000 (16,000 seats).
Record attendance: 41,826 v Tottenham Hotspur, First Division, 20th September, 1969.
Record victory: 12–0 v Finn Harps, UEFA Cup First Round (first leg), 15th September, 1981.
Record defeat: 2–11 v Everton, FA Cup First Round, 1889–90.
Record transfer received: £2,900,000 from Liverpool for Dean Saunders, July 1991.
Record transfer paid: £1,000,000 to Oxford United for Dean Saunders, October 1988.
Honours: League Champions: 1971–72; 1974–75.
Second Division Champions: 1911–12; 1914–15; 1968–69; 1986–87.
Third Division (North) Champions: 1956–57.
FA Cup Winners: 1945–46.

Football League record: 1888 founder member of the Football League; 1907–12 Second Division; 1912–14 First Division; 1914–15 Second Division; 1915–21 First Division; 1921–26 Second Division; 1926–53 First Division; 1953–55 Second Division; 1955–57 Third Division (North); 1957–69 Second Division; 1969–80 First Division; 1980–84 Second Division; 1984–86 Third Division; 1986–87 Second Division; 1987–1991 First Division; 1991– Second Division.

Managers since the War: Stuart McMillan 1946–53; Jack Barker 1953–55; Harry Storer 1955–62; Tim Ward 1962–67; Brian Clough 1967–73; Dave Mackay 1973–76; Colin Murphy 1977; Tommy Docherty 1977–79; Colin Addison 1979–82; Johnny Newman 1982; Peter Taylor 1982–84; Roy McFarland 1984; Arthur Cox 1984– .

Some former famous players: Steve Bloomer; Jack Bowers; Ray Shaw; Kevin Hector; Peter Shilton; Colin Todd; Roy McFarland; Archie Gemmill.

One of the 12 founder members of the Football League in 1888, Derby had been formed by members of the County Cricket Club four years earlier.

From 1895 the football club have played at the Baseball Ground. The ground is so-called because the original owner, foundry boss Francis Ley, became a keen baseball fan following a trip to the United States.

Mr. Ley had the pitch adapted so that his employees could play the game. In fact, several League clubs including Derby County, Aston Villa and Leyton Orient entered baseball teams into a national tournament.

County won the Championship in 1897, with Steve Bloomer, one of their most famous stars of the past, playing at second base.

The club also made a fine start in the Football League, winning 6–3 away at Bolton Wanderers in September 1888.

Derby have played an important role in the game ever since.

DONCASTER ROVERS
Formed: 1879. Turned professional: 1885.
Nickname: Rovers.
Address: Belle Vue Ground, Doncaster.
Telephone: 0302 539441.
ClubCall: 0898 121651.
Manager: Billy Bremner.
Ground capacity: 4,859.
Record attendance: 37,149 v Hull City, Third Division (North), 2nd October, 1948.
Record victory: 10–0 v Darlington, Fourth Division, 25th January, 1964.
Record defeat: 0–12 v Small Heath, Second Division, 11th April, 1903.
Record transfer received: £200,000 from Leeds United for Ian Snodin, May 1985.
Record transfer paid: £60,000 to Stirling Albion for John Philliben, March 1984.
Honours: *Third Division (North) Champions*: 1934–35; 1946–47; 1949–50.
Fourth Division Champions: 1965–66; 1968–69.
Football League record: 1901 elected to Second Division; 1903 failed re-election; 1904 re-elected; 1905 failed re-election; 1923 re-elected to Third Division (North); 1935–37 Second Division; 1937–47 Third Division (North); 1947–48 Second Division; 1948–50 Third Division (North); 1950–58 Second Division; 1958–59 Third Division; 1959–66 Fourth Division; 1966–67 Third Division; 1967–69 Fourth Division; 1969–71 Third Division; 1971–81 Fourth Division; 1981–83 Third Division; 1983–84 Fourth Division; 1984–88 Third Division; 1988– Fourth Division.
Managers since the War: Jackie Bestall 1946–49; Peter Doherty 1949–58; Jack Hodgson and Sid Bycroft (joint managers) 1958; Jack Crayston 1958–59; Jackie Bestall 1959–60; Norman Curtis 1960–61; Danny Malloy 1961–62; Oscar Hold 1962–64; Bill Leivers 1964–66; Keith Kettleborough 1966–67; George Raynor 1967–68; Lawrie McMenemy 1968–71; Maurice Setters 1971–74; Stan Anderson 1975–78; Billy Bremner 1978–85; Dave Cusack 1985–87; Dave Mackay 1987–89; Billy Bremner 1989– .
Some former famous players: Clarrie Jordan; Tom Keetley; Len Graham; Fred Emery.

In 1879, a team was hastily formed to play a game against the Yorkshire Institute for the Deaf. The players enjoyed the match so much that they decided to stay together and call themselves Doncaster Rovers.

Elected to the Second Division in 1901, Rovers drew their first game 3–3 at home to Burslem Port Vale.

Home at the time was the Intake Ground. Rovers moved to Belle Vue in 1922 after the fans had built the pitch and terracing from tons of ash carried from the local coal tips.

The club had the biggest pitch in the League until manager Billy Bremner sliced eight yards from the length some years ago.

EVERTON

Formed: 1878. Turned professional: 1885.
Nickname: The Toffees.
Address: Goodison Park, Liverpool, L4 4EL.
Telephone: 051 521 2020. ClubCall: 0898 121199.
Manager: Howard Kendall.
Ground capacity: 41,366 (29,500 seats).
Record attendance: 78,299 v Liverpool, First Division, 18th September, 1948.
Record victory: 11–2 v Derby County, FA Cup First Round, 18th January, 1890.
Record defeat: 4–10 v Tottenham Hotspur, First Division, 11th October, 1958.
Record transfer received: £2,750,000 from Barcelona for Gary Lineker, July 1986.
Record transfer paid: £2,000,000 to West Ham United for Tony Cottee, July 1988.
Honours: *League Champions*: 1890–91; 1914–15; 1927–28; 1931–32; 1938–39; 1962–63; 1969–70; 1984–85; 1986–87.
Second Division Champions: 1930–31.
FA Cup Winners: 1906; 1933; 1966; 1984.
European Cup-Winners' Cup Winners: 1984–85.
Football League record: 1888 founder member of the Football League; 1930–31 Second Division; 1931–51 First Division; 1951–54 Second Division; 1954– First Division.
Managers since the War: Theo Kelly 1936–48; Cliff Britton 1948–56; Ian Buchan 1956–58; Johnny Carey 1958–61; Harry Catterick 1961–73; Billy Bingham 1973–77; Gordon Lee 1977–81; Howard Kendall 1981–87; Colin Harvey 1987–1990; Howard Kendall 1990– .

Some former famous players: William Ralph; Dixie Dean; Ted Sagar; Alan Ball; Colin Harvey; Howard Kendall; Andy Gray; Gary Lineker.

But for Everton there wouldn't be a Liverpool. It's true! Everton played at Anfield between the years 1884–92 . . . and even won the League Championship during that time. When Everton decided to quit Anfield, a new club was formed . . . Liverpool.

But Everton were born in 1878 when the lads of St. Domingo Church School formed a football team. They played on a pitch in Stanley Park, an area between Anfield and Goodison Park that still exists today.

In 1897, the St.Domingo's team changed their name to Everton.The team was nicknamed The Black Watch by their fans because they played in black shirts. Their famous royal blue livery wasn't introduced until 1901.

An original member of the Football League, Everton won their first game 2–1 at home to Accrington Stanley.

In 1892 the club took over Goodison Park which became the first major soccer stadium in the country.

EXETER CITY

Formed: 1904. Turned professional: 1908.
Nickname: The Grecians.
Address: St. James' Park, Exeter EX4 6PX.
Telephone: 0392 54073. ClubCall: 0898 121634.
Manager: Terry Cooper.
Ground capacity: 17,086.
Record attendance: 20,984 v Sunderland, FA Cup Sixth Round replay, 4th March, 1931.
Record victory: 9–1 v Aberdare, FA Cup First Round, 26th November, 1927.
Record defeat: 0–9 v Notts County, Third Division (South), 16th October, 1948 and v Northampton Town, Third Division (South), 12th April, 1958.
Record transfer received: £105,000 from Blackpool for Tony Kellow, November 1978.
Record transfer paid: £65,000 to Blackpool for Tony Kellow, March 1980.
Honours: *Fourth Division Champions*: 1989–90.

Third Division (South) Cup winners: 1934.
Football League record: 1920 elected to Third Division;
1921–58 Third Division (South); 1958–64 Fourth Division;
1964–66 Third Division; 1966–67 Fourth Division;
1977–84 Third Division; 1984–90 Fourth Division;
1990– Third Division.
Managers since the War: George Roughton 1945–52;
Norman Kirkham 1952–53; Norman Dodgin 1953–57; Bill
Thompson 1957–58; Frank Broome 1958–60; Glen Wilson
1960–62; Cyril Spiers 1962–63; Jack Edwards 1963–65;
Ellis Stuttard 1965–66; Jock Basford 1966–67; Frank
Broome 1967–69; Johnny Newman 1969–76; Bobby
Saxton 1977–79; Brian Godfrey 1979–83; Gerry Francis
1983–84; Jim Iley 1984–85; Colin Appleton 1985–87; Terry
Cooper 1988– .
Some former famous players: Fred Whitlow; Dermot
Curtis; Arnold Mitchell.

Formed in 1904 by the players of St. Sidwell's United and
Exeter United. They turned professional four years later
and joined the Southern League.
    Elected to the Third Division in 1920, Exeter defeated
Brentford 3-0 at home in their first match.
    During the Second World War, the ground was used to
house American troops.

FULHAM

Formed: 1879. Turned professional:
1898.
Nickname: The Cottagers.
Address: Craven Cottage, Stevenage
Road, Fulham, London SW6.
Telephone: 071 736 6561. ClubCall:
0898 121198.
Manager: Alan Dicks.
Ground capacity: 18,304.
Record attendance: 49,335 v
Millwall, Second Division, 8th
October, 1938.
Record victory: 10–1 v Ipswich
Town, First Division, 26th
December, 1963.
Record defeat: 0–10 v Liverpool, League Cup Second
Round (first leg), 23rd September, 1986.
Record transfer received: £333,333 from Liverpool for
Richard Money, May 1980.

Record transfer paid: £150,000 to Orient for Peter Kitchen, February 1979 and to Brighton & Hove Albion for Teddy Maybank, December 1979.

Honours: *Second Division Champions*: 1948–49.

Third Division (South) Champions: 1931–32.

Football League record: 1907 elected to the Second Division; 1928–32 Third Division (South); 1932–49 Second Division; 1949–52 First Division; 1952–59 Second Division; 1959–68 First Division; 1968–69 Second Division; 1969–71 Third Division; 1971–80 Second Division; 1980–82 Third Division; 1982–86 Second Division; 1986– Third Division.

Managers since the War: Jack Peart 1935–48; Frank Osbourne 1948–64 (secretary-manager and GM for most of that period); Bill Dodgin Snr 1949–53; Duggie Livingstone 1956–58; Bedford Jezzard 1958–64; Vic Buckingham 1965–68; Bobby Robson 1968; Bill Dodgin Jnr 1969–72; Alec Stock 1972–76; Bobby Campbell 1976–80; Malcolm Macdonald 1980–84; Ray Harford 1984–86; Ray Lewington 1986–90; Alan Dicks 1990– .

Some former famous players: Frank Newton; Bedford Jezzard; Johnny Haynes; Bobby Robson; Ron Greenwood; Tony Macedo; George Cohen; Alan Mullery; Rodney Marsh; George Best; Bobby Moore.

The club began as Fulham St. Andrew's Church Sunday School FC in 1879. They decided to call themselves Fulham in 1888, the year the Football League was introduced.

They joined the Second Division in 1907, losing their first game 1–0 away at Hull City.

In 1961, when the maximum wage (£20) for footballers was abolished, Fulham's legendary star Johnny Haynes became Britain's first £100-a-week player.

GILLINGHAM

Formed: 1893. Turned professional: 1894.

Nickname: The Gills.

Address: Priestfield Stadium, Gillingham.

Telephone: 0634 51854. ClubCall: 0898 121107.

Manager: Damien Richardson.

Ground capacity: 19,581.

Record attendance: 23,002 v QPR, FA Cup Third Round, 10th January, 1948.

Record victory: 10–0 v Chesterfield, Third Division, 5th September, 1987.

Record defeat: 2–9 v Nottingham Forest, Third Division (South), 18th November, 1950.

Record transfer received: £250,000 from Bournemouth for Gavin Peacock, August 1989.

Record transfer paid: £102,500 to Tottenham Hotspur for Mark Cooper, October 1987.

Honours: *Fourth Division Champions*: 1963–64.

Football League record: 1920 original member of Third Division; 1921 Third Division (South); 1938 failed re-election; Southern League 1938–44; Kent League 1944–46; Southern League 1946–50; 1950 re-elected to Third Division (South); 1958–64 Fourth Division; 1964–71 Third Division; 1971–74 Fourth Division; 1974–89 Third Division; 1989– Fourth Division.

Managers since the War: Archie Clark 1939–58; Harry Barratt 1958–62; Freddie Cox 1962–65; Basil Hayward 1966–71; Andy Nelson 1971–74; Len Ashurst 1974–75; Gerry Summers 1975–81; Keith Peacock 1981–87; Paul Taylor 1988; Keith Burkinshaw 1988–89; Damien Richardson 1989– .

Some former famous players: Ernie Morgan; Brian Yeo; John Simpson; Tony Cascarino.

The FA Cup exploits of the Chatham based Royal Engineers during the 1870's encouraged the start of many football clubs in the Medway area of Kent, including Excelsior.

After winning the Kent Junior Cup and Chatham District League in 1893, Excelsior decided to turn professional at a meeting in the Napier Arms, Brompton.

So New Brompton was formed. The club played under that name until 1913 when they adopted their present name of Gillingham FC.

They were founder members of the Third Division in 1920 and drew their first League match 1-1 at home to Southampton.

GRIMSBY TOWN

Formed: 1878. Turned professional: 1890.
Nickname: The Mariners.
Address: Blundell Park, Cleethorpes, South Humberside. DN35 7PY.
Telephone: 0472 697111.
ClubCall: 0898 121576.
Manager: Alan Buckley.
Ground capacity: 18,496.
Record attendance: 31,651 v Wolverhampton Wanderers, FA Cup Fifth Round, 20th February, 1937.
Record victory: 8–0 v Darlington, FA Cup Second Round, 21st November, 1885.
Record defeat: 1–9 v Arsenal, First Division, 28th January, 1931.
Record transfer received: £300,000 from Everton for Paul Wilkinson, March 1985.
Record transfer paid: £110,000 to Watford for James Gilligan, July 1985.
Honours: *Second Division Champions*: 1900–01; 1933–34.
Third Division (North) Champions: 1925–26; 1955–56.
Third Division Champions: 1979–80.
Fourth Division Champions: 1971–72.
League Group Cup winners: 1981–82.
Football League record: 1892 original member of Second Division; 1901–03 First Division; 1903 Second Division; 1910 failed re-election; 1911 re-elected to Second Division; 1920–21 Third Division; 1921–26 Third Division (North); 1926–29 Second Division; 1929–32 First Division; 1932–34 Second Division; 1934–48 First Division; 1948–51 Second Division; 1951–56 Third Division (North); 1956–59 Second Division; 1959–62 Third Division; 1962–64 Second Division; 1964–68 Third Division; 1968–72 Fourth Division; 1972–77 Third Division; 1977–79 Fourth Division; 1979–80 Third Division; 1980–87 Second Division; 1987–88 Third Division; 1988–90 Fourth Division; 1990–91 Third Division; 1991– Second Division.
Managers since the War: Charles Spencer 1937–51; Bill Shankly 1951–53; Billy Walsh 1954–55; Allenby Chilton

1955–59; Tim Ward 1960–62; Tom Johnston 1962–64; Jimmy McGuigan 1964–67; Don McEvoy 1967–68; Bill Harvey 1968–69; Bobby Kennedy 1969–71; Lawrie McMenemy 1971–73; Ron Ashman 1973–75; Tom Casey 1975–76; Johnny Newman 1976–79; George Kerr 1979–82; David Booth 1982–85; Mike Lyons 1985–87; Bobby Roberts 1987–88; Alan Buckley 1988– .
Some former famous players: Pat Glover; Keith Jobling.

First known as Grimsby Pelham FC when the club was formed in 1878. Pelham was the name of a wealthy family in the area.

A year later the club changed their name to Grimsby Town. They were founder members of the Second Division in 1892, winning their first League match 2–1 at home to Northwich Victoria.

HALIFAX TOWN

Formed: 1911. Turned professional: 1911.
Nickname: The Shaymen.
Address: Shay Ground, Halifax. HX1 2YS.
Telephone: 0422 53423.
Manager: Jim McCalliog.
Ground capacity: 5,656.
Record attendance: 36,885 v Tottenham Hotspur, FA Cup Fifth Round, 15th February, 1953.
Record victory: 7–0 v Bishop Auckland, FA Cup Second Round replay, 10th January, 1967.
Record defeat: 0–13 v Stockport County, Third Division (North), 6th January 1934.
Record transfer received: £250,000 from Watford for Wayne Allison, July 1989.
Record transfer paid: £40,000 to Leyton Orient for Ian Juryeff, August 1989.
Honours: None.
Football League record: 1921 original member of Third Division (North); 1958–63 Third Division; 1963–69 Fourth Division; 1969–76 Third Division; 1976– Fourth Division.
Managers since the War: Jack Breedon 1947–50; William Wootton 1951–52; Gerald Henry 1952–54; Willie Watson 1954–56; Billy Burnikell 1956; Harry Hooper 1957–62; Willie Watson 1964–66; Vic Metcalfe 1966–67; Alan Ball Snr 1967–70; George Kirby 1970–71; Ray Henderson

1971–72; George Mulhall 1972–74; Johnny Quinn 1974–76;
Alan Ball Snr 1976–77; Jimmy Lawson 1977–78; George
Kirby 1978–81; Mick Bullock 1981–84; Mick Jones
1984–86; Bill Ayre 1986–90; Jim McCalliog 1990– .
Some former famous players: Albert Valentine; Ernest
Dixon; John Pickering.

First formed in May 1911 after an article appealing for the
introduction of a football club in a town renowned for
Rugby League appeared in the Halifax Evening Courier.

Halifax became a founder member of the Third Division
(North) in 1921, losing their first game 2–0 away at
Darlington.

HARTLEPOOL UNITED
Formed: 1908. Turned professional:
1908.
Nickname: The Pool.
Address: The Victoria Ground,
Clarence Road, Hartlepool.
Telephone: 0429 272584. ClubCall:
0898 121147.
Manager: Cyril Knowles.
Ground capacity: 9,675.
Record attendance: 17,426 v
Manchester United, FA Cup Third
Round, 5th January, 1957.
Record victory: 10–1 v Barrow,
Fourth Division, 4th April, 1959.
Record defeat: 1–10 v Wrexham, Fourth Division, 3rd
March, 1962.
Record transfer received: £175,000 from Liverpool for
Don Hutchinson, November 1990.
Record transfer paid: £17,500 to Chesterfield for Bob
Newton, July 1985.
Honours: None.
Football League record: 1921 original member of Third
Division (North); 1958–68 Fourth Division; 1968–69 Third
Division; 1969–91 Fourth Division; 1991– Third Division.
Managers since the War: Fred Westgarth 1943–57; Ray
Middleton 1957–59; Bill Robinson 1959–62; Allenby
Chilton 1962–63; Bob Gurney 1963–64; Alvan Williams
1964–65; Geoff Twentyman 1965; Brian Clough 1965–67;
Angus McLean 1967–70; John Simpson 1970–71; Len
Ashurst 1971–74; Ken Hale 1974–76; Billy Horner
1976–83; Johnny Duncan 1983; Mike Docherty 1983; Billy
Horner 1984–86; John Bird 1986–88; Bobby Moncur

1988–89; Cyril Knowles 1989– .
Some former famous players: William Robinson; Ken
Johnston; Ambrose Fogerty; Wattie Moore.

The FA Amateur Cup Final triumph of West Hartlepool in
1905 inspired the formation of a new club three years later.
They called themselves Hartlepools United, retaining the
's' until 1968.
   The club became a founder member of the Third
Division (North) in 1921, winning their first League game
2–0 at Wrexham.

HEREFORD UNITED

Formed: 1924. Turned professional:
1924.
Nickname: United.
Address: Edgar Street, Hereford.
Telephone: 0432 276666.
ClubCall: 0898 121645.
Manager: John Sillett.
Ground capacity: 13,777.
Record attendance: 18,114 v Sheffield
Wednesday, FA Cup Third Round,
28th January, 1958.
Record victory: 6–0 v Burnley,
Fourth Division, 24th January, 1987.
Record defeat: 0–6 v Rotherham
United, Fourth Division, 29th April, 1989.
Record transfer received: £175,000 from Notts County for
Phil Stant, July 1989.
Record transfer paid: £50,000 to Halifax Town for Ian
Juryeff, December 1989.
Honours: *Third Division Champions*: 1975–76.
Welsh Cup Winners: 1990.
Football League record: 1972 elected to the Fourth
Division; 1973–77 Third Division; 1976–77 Second
Division; 1977–78 Third Division; 1978– Fourth Division.
Managers since the War: George Tranter 1948–49; Alex
Massie 1952; George Tranter 1953–55; Joe Wade 1956–62;
Ray Daniels 1962–63; Bob Dennison 1963—67; John
Charles 1967–71; Colin Addison 1971–74; John Sillett
1974–78; Mike Bailey 1978–79; Frank Lord 1979–82;
Tommy Hughes 1982–83; Johnny Newman 1983–87; Ian
Bowyer 1987–90; Colin Addison 1990–91; John Sillett
1991– .
Some former famous players: Dixie McNeil; Brian Evans;
Mike Pejic.

Formed in 1924 when several local clubs amalgamated.

Hereford City, the town's leading club allowed United to share their Edgar Street ground.

City ceased to exist as a club just before the outbreak of the Second World War and United went on to establish themselves in the Southern League.

United's FA Cup exploits helped them gain entry into the Football League in 1972 to replace Barrow.

They lost their first League match 1–0 away at Colchester United.

HUDDERSFIELD TOWN

Formed: 1908. Turned professional: 1908.
Nickname: The Terriers.
Address: Leeds Road, Huddersfield. HD1 6PE.
Telephone: 0484 420335. ClubCall: 0898 121635.
Manager: Eoin Hand.
Ground capacity: 32,000.
Record attendance: 67,037 v Arsenal, FA Cup Sixth Round, 27th February, 1932.
Record victory: 10–1 v Blackpool, First Division, 13th December, 1930.
Record defeat: 1–10 v Manchester City, Second Division, 7th November, 1987.
Record transfer received: £230,000 from Swindon Town for Duncan Shearer, June 1988.
Record transfer paid: £110,000 to Mansfield Town for Terry Austin, December 1980.
Honours: *League Champions*: 1923–24; 1924–25; 1925–26.
Second Division Champions: 1969–70.
Fourth Division Champions: 1979–80.
FA Cup Winners: 1921–22.
Football League record: 1910 elected to Second Division; 1920–52 First Division; 1952–53 Second Division; 1953–56 First Division; 1956–70 Second Division; 1970–72 First Division; 1972–73 Second Division; 1973–75 Third Division; 1975–80 Fourth Division; 1980–83 Third Division; 1983–88 Second Division; 1988– Third Division.
Managers since the War: George Stephenson 1947–52; Andy Beattie 1952–56; Bill Shankly 1956–59; Eddie Boot 1960–64; Tom Johnston 1964–68; Ian Greaves 1968–74;

Bobby Collins 1974; Tom Johnston 1975–78; Mike Buxton 1978–86; Steve Smith 1986–87; Malcolm Macdonald 1987–88; Eoin Hand 1988– .
Some former famous players: Sam Taylor; George Brown; Jimmy Glazzard; Billy Smith; Frank Goodall; Vic Metcalfe; Roy Staniforth; Jimmy Nicholson.

Formed in 1908, the club rented the Leeds Road ground from the local authority. Facilities were so primitive that the players were forced to change in an old tramcar and the spectators sat on uncovered wooden seats.

Two years later Town joined the Football League, winning their first game 1–0 away at Bradford Park Avenue.

Shortly after the First World War, a financial crisis almost forced the club out of business.

Massive fund raising and demonstrations by the fans kept the club alive. It not only survived but thrived sensationally!

Within a few years Huddersfield had won the League Championship three seasons in succession and the FA Cup.

HULL CITY

Formed: 1904. Turned professional: 1905.
Nickname: The Tigers.
Address: Boothferry Park, Hull. HU4 6EU.
Telephone: 0482 51119.
Manager: Terry Dolan.
Ground capacity: 17,932.
Record attendance: 55,019 v Manchester United, FA Cup Sixth Round, 26th February, 1949.
Record victory: 11–1 v Carlisle United, Third Division (North), 14th January, 1939.
Record defeat: 0–8 v Wolverhampton Wanderers, Second Division, 4th November, 1911.
Record transfer received: £400,000 from Sunderland for Tony Norman, December 1988.
Record transfer paid: £200,000 to Leeds United for Peter Swan, March 1989.
Honours: *Third Division (North) Champions*: 1932–33; 1948–49.
Third Division Champions: 1965–66.

Football League record: 1905 elected to Second Division; 1930–33 Third Division (North); 1933–36 Second Division; 1936–49 Third Division (North); 1949–56 Second Division; 1956–58 Third Division (North); 1958–59 Third Division; 1959–60 Second Division; 1960–66 Third Division; 1966–78 Second Division; 1978–81 Third Division; 1981–83 Fourth Division; 1983–85 Third Division; 1985– Second Division; 1991– Third Division.

Managers since the War: Major Frank Buckley 1946–48; Raich Carter 1948–51; Bob Jackson 1952–55; Bob Brocklebank 1955–61; Cliff Britton 1961–70; Terry Neill 1970–74; John Kaye 1974–77; Bobby Collins 1977–78; Ken Houghton 1978–79; Mike Smith 1979–82; Bobby Brown 1982; Colin Appleton 1982–84; Brian Horton 1984–88; Eddie Gray 1988–89; Colin Appleton 1989; Stan Ternent 1989–91; Terry Dolan 1991– .

Some former famous players: Bill McNaughton; Chris Chilton; Terry Neill; Andy Davidson.

When formed in 1904, Hull City caused something of a sensation by sharing their home ground with Hull Rugby League Club.

They were Elected to the Second Division a year later, defeating Barnsley 4–1 at home in their first game.

IPSWICH TOWN
Formed: 1878. Turned professional: 1936.
Nickname: The Blues or Town.
Address: Portman Road, Ipswich, Suffolk, 1P1 2DA.
Telephone: 0473 219211.
Manager: John Lyall.
Ground capacity: 31,000.
Record attendance: 38,010 v Leeds United, FA Cup Sixth Round, 8th March, 1975.

Record victory: 10–0 v Floriana, European Cup, Preliminary Round, 25th September, 1962.
Record defeat: 1–10 v Fulham, First Division, 26th December, 1963.
Record transfer received: £725,000 from Glasgow Rangers for Terry Butcher, August 1986.
Record transfer paid: £330,000 to Manchester City for Brian Gayle, January 1990.
Honours: *League Champions*: 1961–62.

Second Division Champions: 1960–61; 1967–68. *Third Division (South) Champions*: 1953–54; 1956–57.
FA Cup Winners: 1977–78.
UEFA Cup Winners: 1980–81.
Football League record: 1938 elected to Third Division (South); 1954–55 Second Division; 1955–57 Third Division (South); 1957–61 Second Division; 1961–64 First Division; 1964–68 Second Division; 1968–86 First Division; 1986– Second Division.
Managers since the War: Scott Duncan 1937–55; Alf Ramsey 1955–63; Jackie Milburn 1963–64; Bill McGarry 1964–68; Bobby Robson 1969–82; Bobby Ferguson 1982–87; Johnny Duncan 1987–90; John Lyall 1990– .
Some former famous players: Ted Phillips; Ray Crawford; Roy Bailey; Jimmy Leadbetter; Brian Talbot; Dave Johnson; Allan Hunter; Mick Mills; Paul Mariner; John Wark; Frans Thijssen; Arnold Muhren; Terry Butcher.

Formed in 1878 after a meeting held in the Ipswich Town Hall and a Mr. T. C. Cobbold M.P. was elected President. Members of the Cobbold family have been connected with the club ever since.

Ten years later the football club amalgamated with Ipswich Rugby Club until 1893 when they abandoned the oval ball game completely.

Elected to the Third Division (South) in 1938, Town won their first League game, 4–2 at home to Southend United.

LEEDS UNITED

Formed: 1919. Turned professional: 1920.
Nickname: United or The Whites.
Address: Elland Road, Leeds, LS11 0ES.
Telephone: 0532 716037. ClubCall: 0898 121180.
Manager: Howard Wilkinson.
Ground capacity: 40,176.
Record attendance: 57,892 v Sunderland, FA Cup Fifth Round replay, 15th March, 1967.
Record victory: 10–0 v Lyn Oslo, European Cup, First Round (first leg), 17th September, 1969.
Record defeat: 1–8 v Stoke City, First Division, 27th August, 1934.

Record transfer received: £825,000 from Everton for Ian Snodin, January 1987.

Record transfer paid: £1,000,000 to Arsenal for John Lukic, May 1990 and to Leicester City for Gary McAllister, June 1990.

Honours: *League Champions*: 1968-69; 1973-74.

Second Division Champions: 1923-24; 1963-64; 1989-90.

FA Cup Winners: 1971-72.

Football League Cup Winners: 1967-68.

European Fairs Cup (now UEFA Cup) Winners: 1967-68; 1970-71.

Football League record: 1920 elected to Second Division; 1924-27 First Division; 1927-28 Second Division; 1928-31 First Division; 1931-32 Second Division; 1932-47 First Division; 1947-56 Second Division; 1956-60 First Division; 1960-64 Second Division; 1964-82 First Division; 1982-90 Second Division; 1990- First Division.

Managers since the War: Willis Edwards 1947-48; Major Frank Buckley 1948-53; Raich Carter 1953-58; Bill Lambton 1958-59; Jack Taylor 1959-61; Don Revie 1961-74; Brian Clough 1974; Jimmy Armfield 1974-78; Jock Stein 1978; Jimmy Adamson 1978-80; Allan Clarke 1980-82; Eddie Gray 1982-85; Billy Bremner 1985-88; Howard Wilkinson 1988- .

Some former famous players: John Charles; Peter Lorimer; Billy Bremner; Jack Charlton; Norman Hunter; John Giles; Paul Madeley; Terry Cooper.

The club was reformed as Leeds United in 1919, after Leeds City (formed 1904) was disbanded by the FA following allegations of illegal payments to players.

A few weeks later, in a desperate effort to ease their financial problems, Huddersfield Town suggested the two clubs amalgamate. The idea never got off the ground and both clubs went on to achieve top honours.

Leeds were elected to the Second Division in 1920. Unfortunately, they lost their first League game 2-0 at Port Vale.

LEICESTER CITY

Formed: 1884. Turned professional: 1894.

Nickname: The Filberts or The Foxes.

Address: City Stadium, Filbert Street, Leicester. LE2 7FL.

Telephone: 0533 555000. ClubCall: 0898 121185.

Manager: Brian Little

Ground capacity: 31,000.

Record attendance: 47,298 v Tottenham Hotspur, FA Cup Fifth Round, 18th February, 1928.

Record victory: 10–0 v Portsmouth, First Division, 20th October, 1928.

Record defeat: 0–12 v Nottingham Forest, First Division, 21st April, 1909.

Record transfer received: £1,050,000 from Everton for Gary Lineker, July 1985.

Record transfer paid: £500,000 to Everton for Wayne Clarke, July 1989.

Honours: *Second Division Champions*: 1924–25; 1936–37; 1953–54; 1956–57; 1970–71; 1979–80.

Football League Cup Winners: 1963–64.

Football League record: 1894 elected to Second Division; 1908–09 First Division; 1909–25 Second Division; 1925–35 First Division; 1935–37 Second Division; 1937–39 First Division; 1946–54 Second Division; 1954–55 First Division; 1955–57 Second Division; 1957–69 First Division; 1969–71 Second Division; 1971–78 First Division; 1978–80 Second Division; 1980–81 First Division; 1981–83 Second Division; 1983–87 First Division; 1987– Second Division.

Managers since the War: Johnny Duncan 1946–49; Norman Bullock 1949–55; David Halliday 1955–58; Matt Gillies 1959–68; Frank O'Farrell 1968–71; Jimmy Bloomfield 1971–77; Frank McLintock 1977–78; Jock Wallace 1978–82; Gordon Milne 1982–86; Bryan Hamilton 1986–87; David Pleat 1987–91; Brian Little 1991– .

Some former famous players: Arthur Chandler; Arthur Rowley; Adam Black; Gordon Banks; Gary Lineker.

Formed in 1884 when several old boys of Wyggeston School got together and arranged a meeting in a house on Fosse Way. As a result of the location they decided to call themselves Leicester Fosse.

Two years later the club signed their first professional player, Harry Webb from Stafford Rangers for the princely sum of 2s.6d a week (just over 12p) plus travelling expenses.

They had to pay Gary Lineker, one of the club's most famous former stars, a great deal more than that in the 1980's.

Leicester were elected to the Second Division in 1894. They lost their first League match 4–3 away at Grimsby Town.

LEYTON ORIENT

Formed: 1881. Turned professional: 1903.
Nickname: The O's.
Address: Leyton Stadium, Brisbane Road, Leyton, London E10 5NE.
Telephone: 081 539 2223. ClubCall: 0898 121150.
Manager: Frank Clark.
Ground capacity: 18,869 (7,171 seats).
Record attendance: 34,345 v West Ham United, FA Cup Fourth Round, 25th January, 1964.
Record victory: 8–0 v Crystal Palace, Third Division (South), 12th November, 1955.
Record defeat: 0–8 v Aston Villa, FA Cup Fourth Round, 30th January, 1929.
Record transfer received: £600,000 from Notts County for John Chiedozie, August 1981.
Record transfer paid: £175,000 to Wigan Athletic for Paul Beesley, October 1989.
Honours: *Third Division Champions*: 1969–70.
Third Division (South) Champions: 1955–56.
Football League record: 1905 elected to Second Division; 1929–56 Third Division (South); 1956–62 Second Division; 1962–63 First Division; 1963–66 Second Division; 1966–70 Third Division; 1970–82 Second Division; 1982–85 Third Division; 1985–89 Fourth Division; 1989– Third Division.
Managers since the War: Charlie Hewitt 1946–48; Neil McBain 1948–49; Alec Stock 1949–59; Johnny Carey 1961–63; Benny Fenton 1963–64; Dave Sexton 1965; Dick Graham 1966–68; Jimmy Bloomfield 1968–71; George Petchey 1971–77; Jimmy Bloomfield 1977–81; Paul Went 1981; Ken Knighton 1981; Frank Clark 1982– .
Some former famous players: Tom Johnston; Peter Allen; Phil Woosnam; David Webb; John Chiedozie.

Formed in 1881 when students of Homerton Theological College and members of Glyn Cricket Club decided to play football throughout the winter months.

Seven years later, employees of the Orient Shipping Line joined the team. After a meeting it was decided to rename the club Orient FC.

They were elected to the Second Division in 1905 and lost their first League game 2–1 away at Leicester Fosse.

During the early Sixties the club reached their peak and enjoyed a season in the First Division, a period when they attracted a strong show-biz following.

LINCOLN CITY
Formed: 1883. Turned professional: 1892.
Nickname: The Red Imps.
Address: Sincil Bank, Lincoln. LN5 8LD.
Telephone: 0522 522224. ClubCall: 0898 121889.
Manager: Steve Thompson.
Ground capacity: 10,369.
Record attendance: 23,196 v Derby County, League Cup Fourth Round, 15th November, 1967.
Record victory: 11–1 v Crewe Alexandra, Third Division (North), 29th September, 1951.
Record defeat: 3–11 v Manchester City, Second Division, 23rd March, 1895.
Record transfer received: £180,000 from Newcastle United for Mick Harford, December 1980.
Record transfer paid: £60,000 to Southampton for Gordon Hobson, September 1988.
Honours: *Third Division (North) Champions*: 1931–32; 1947–48; 1951–52.
Fourth Division Champions: 1975–76.
Football League record: 1892 founder member of Second Division; remained in Second Division until 1920 when they failed re-election. Also failed re-election in 1908–09 and 1911–12; 1921–32 Third Division (North); 1932–34 Second Division; 1934–48 Third Division (North); 1948–49 Second Division; 1949–52 Third Division (North); 1952–61 Second Division; 1961–62 Third Division; 1962–76 Fourth Division; 1976–79 Third Division; 1979–81 Fourth Division; 1981–86 Third Division; 1986–87 Fourth

Division; 1987–88 GM Vauxhall Conference;
1988– Fourth Division.
Managers since the War: Bill Anderson 1946–65; Roy
Chapman 1965–66; Ron Gray 1966–70; Bert Loxley
1970–71; David Herd 1971–72; Graham Taylor 1972–77;
George Kerr 1977–78; Willie Bell 1977–78; Colin Murphy
1978–85; John Pickering 1985; George Kerr 1985–87; Peter
Daniel 1987; Colin Murphy 1987–90; Allan Clarke
1990–91; Steve Thompson 1991– .
Some former famous players: Allan Hall; Andy Graver;
David Pugh; Tom Emery.

The records show that a Lincoln FC were playing around
the 1860's. But the present club was formed in 1883.
    In the early days, the club played on a ground known as
Cow Pat because a local farmer grazed his cattle there.
    Lincoln City kicked off their Football League career in
September 1892, as founder members of the Second
Division.
    They lost their first match, 4–2 away at Sheffield United.

LIVERPOOL

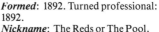

Formed: 1892. Turned professional:
1892.
Nickname: The Reds or The Pool.
Address: Anfield Road, Liverpool 4.
Telephone: 051 262 2361. ClubCall:
0898 121184.
Manager: Graeme Souness.
Ground capacity: 39,772.
Record attendance: 61,905 v
Wolverhampton Wanderers,
FA Cup Fourth Round, 2nd
February, 1952.
Record victory: 11–0 v Stromsgodset
Drammen, European Cup Winners'
Cup, First Round (first leg), 17th September, 1974.
Record defeat: 1–9 v Birmingham City, Second Division,
11th December, 1954.
Record transfer received: £3,200,000 from Juventus for
Ian Rush, June 1986.
Record transfer paid: £2,900,000 to Derby County for
Dean Saunders, July 1991.
Honours: *League Champions*: 1900–01; 1905–06;
1921–22; 1922–23; 1946–47; 1963–64; 1965–66; 1972–73;
1975–76; 1976–77; 1978–79; 1979–80; 1981–82; 1982–83;

1983–84; 1985–86; 1987–88; 1989–90 (a record 18 League titles).
Second Division Champions: 1893–94; 1895–96; 1904–05; 1961–62.
FA Cup Winners: 1965; 1974; 1986; 1989.
Football League Cup Winners: 1981; 1982; 1983; 1984.
League Super Cup Winners: 1985–86.
European Cup Winners: 1976–77; 1977–78; 1980–81; 1983–84.
UEFA Cup Winners: 1972–73; 1975–76.
Super Cup Winners: 1977.
Football League record: 1893 elected to Second Division; 1894–95 First Division; 1895–96 Second Division; 1896–1904 First Division; 1905–05 Second Division; 1905–54 First Division; 1954–62 Second Division; 1962– First Division.
Managers since the War: George Kay 1936–51; Don Welsh 1951–56; Phil Taylor 1956–59; Bill Shankly 1959–74; Bob Paisley 1974–83; Joe Fagan 1983–85; Kenny Dalglish 1985–91; Ronnie Moran (acting manager) 1991; Graeme Souness 1991– .
Some former famous players: Albert Stubbins; Tommy Lawrence; Ron Yeats; Roger Hunt; Emlyn Hughes; Phil Thompson; Ray Clemence; Ian Callaghan; Tommy Smith.

But for a dispute between Everton FC and the owners of their home ground Anfield in 1892, Liverpool would probably not exist today. When Everton finally quit Anfield for Goodison Park, a new club Liverpool Association FC was formed.

Liverpool joined the Second Division in 1893 and won their first game, 2–0 away at Middlesbrough.

The club achieved their first Championship triumph seven years later. Liverpool have broken records ever since to become one of the most famous and successful clubs in the world.

LUTON TOWN
Formed: 1885. Turned professional: 1890.
Nickname: The Hatters.
Address: Kenilworth Road Stadium, 1 Maple Road, Luton, Beds. LU4 8AW.
Telephone: 0582 411622.
Manager: David Pleat.
Ground capacity: 13,023.
Record attendance: 30,069 v Blackpool, FA Cup Sixth Round replay, 4th March, 1959.
Record victory: 12–0 v Bristol Rovers, Third Division (South), 13th April, 1936.
Record defeat: 0–9 v Small Heath, Second Division, 12th November, 1898.
Record transfer received: £1,000,000 from QPR for Roy Wegerle, December 1989.
Record transfer paid: £850,000 to Odense for Lars Elstrup, August 1989.
Honours: *Second Division Champions*: 1981–82.
Fourth Division Champions: 1967–68.
Third Division (South) Champions: 1936–37.
Football League Cup Winners: 1987–88.
Football League record: 1897 elected to Second Division; 1900 failed re-election; 1920–37 Third Division (South); 1937–55 Second Division; 1955–60 First Division; 1960–63 Second Division; 1963–65 Third Division; 1965–68 Fourth Division; 1968–70 Third Division; 1970–74 Second Division; 1974–75 First Division; 1975–82 Second Division; 1982– First Division.
Managers since the War: George Martin 1939–47; Dally Duncan 1947–58; Syd Owen 1959–60; Sam Bartram 1960–62; Bill Harvey 1962–64; George Martin 1965–66; Allan Brown 1966–68; Alec Stock 1968–72; Harry Haslam 1972–78; David Pleat 1978–86; John Moore 1986–87; Ray Harford 1987–89; Jim Ryan 1990–91; David Pleat 1991–.
Some former famous players: Joe Payne; Gordon Turner; Bob Morton; Ron Baynham; Mal Donaghy.

Formed in April 1885 when two local clubs Wanderers and Excelsior held a meeting in Luton Town Hall and agreed to amalgamate.

They were elected to the Second Division twelve years later.

Luton drew their first League match 1-1 away at
Leicester Fosse.
  Installed an artificial surface a couple of years ago.

MAIDSTONE UNITED
Formed: 1891. Turned professional:
1897; reverted to amateur status
1927; became professional again:
1971.
Nickname: The Stones.
Address: Watling Street, Dartford,
Kent. DA2 6EN.
Telephone: 0622 754403.
Manager: Graham Carr.
Ground capacity: 5,250.
Record attendance (at The Stadium,
London Road, Maidstone): 10,591 v
Charlton Athletic, FA Cup Third
Round replay, 15th January, 1979.
Record victory: 5-1 v Aldershot, Fourth Division, 1st
January, 1990.
Record defeat: 1-4 v Colchester United, Fourth Division,
26th September, 1989.
Record transfer received: £150,000 from Watford for
Steve Butler, March 1991.
Record transfer paid: £35,000 to Fisher Athletic for Ken
Charlery, March 1989.
Honours: None.
Football League record: 1989 promoted to Fourth
Division.
Managers since joining the Football League: John Still
1987-89; Keith Peacock 1989-1991; Graham Carr 1991- .
Some former famous players: Steve Butler; Mark Golley.

Formed as Maidstone Invicta in 1891, they played in the
local amateur Kent League.
  In 1897 the club decided to change their name to
Maidstone United and go professional.
  They reverted to an amateur club in the late 1920's when
competing in the then powerful Athenian and Isthmian
Leagues.
  United turned professional again in 1971 when they
joined the Southern League.
  Promoted to the Fourth Division after ending the
1988-89 season as Champions of the GM Vauxhall
Conference. Forced to leave their home ground in London
Road because it failed to meet the required League

standard. They now share Dartford's pitch.

Maidstone's first League match ended in a 1–0 defeat at Peterborough United.

MANCHESTER CITY

Formed: 1887 as Ardwick FC. 1894 as Manchester City. Turned professional: 1887.
Nickname: The Blues.
Address: Maine Road, Moss Side, Manchester. M14 7WN.
Telephone: 061 226 1191. ClubCall: 0898 121191.
Manager: Peter Reid.
Ground capacity: 48,500.
Record attendance: 84,569 v Stoke City, FA Cup Sixth Round, 3rd March, 1934.
Record victory: 10–1 v Huddersfield Town, Second Division, 7th November, 1987 and v Swindon Town, FA Cup Fourth Round, 29th January, 1930.
Record defeat: 1–9 v Everton, First Division, 3rd September, 1906.
Record transfer received: £1,700,000 from Tottenham Hotspur for Paul Stewart, June 1988.
Record transfer paid: £1,437,500 to Wolverhampton Wanderers for Steve Daley, September 1979.
Honours: *League Champions*: 1936–37; 1967–68.
Second Division Champions: 1898–99; 1902–03; 1909–10; 1927–28; 1946–47; 1965–66.
FA Cup Winners: 1904; 1934; 1956; 1969.
Football League Cup Winners: 1970; 1976.
European Cup Winners' Cup Winners: 1969–70.
Football League record: 1892 Ardwick elected original member of Second Division; 1894 Manchester City elected to Second Division; First Division 1899–1902; 1902–03 Second Division; 1903–09 First Division; 1909–10 Second Division; 1910–26 First Division; 1926–28 Second Division; 1928–38 First Division; 1938–47 Second Division; 1947–50 First Division; 1950–51 Second Division; 1951–63 First Division; 1963–66 Second Division; 1966–83 First Division; 1983–85 Second Division; 1985–87 First Division; 1987–89 Second Division; 1989– First Division.
Managers since the War: Sam Cowan 1946–47; John 'Jock' Thompson 1947–50; Leslie McDowall 1950–63; George Poyser 1963–65; Joe Mercer 1965–71; Malcolm Allison 1972–73; Johnny Hart 1973; Ron Saunders

1973–74; Tony Book 1974–79; Malcolm Allison 1979–80; John Bond 1980–83; John Benson 1983; Billy McNeill 1983–86; Jimmy Frizzell 1986–87; Mel Machin 1987–89; Howard Kendall 1989–90; Peter Reid 1990– .
Some former famous players: Tommy Johnson; Frank Swift; Matt Busby; Bert Trautmann; Colin Bell; Tony Book; Joe Corrigan; Francis Lee; Alan Oakes; Peter Barnes; Trevor Francis; Mike Summerbee.

The club began in 1880 when St. Mark's Church, West Gorton formed a football team.

Four years later they amalgamated with Gorton Athletic and changed their name to Gorton FC.

In 1887 they moved to a new home ground and became Ardwick FC. They were elected founder members of the Second Division in 1892, winning their first League match 7–0 at home to Bootle.

Reformed as Manchester City in 1894 when Ardwick were forced into liquidation through bankruptcy.

MANSFIELD TOWN

Formed: 1910. Turned professional: 1910.
Nickname: The Stags.
Address: Field Mill Ground, Quarry Lane, Mansfield.
Telephone: 0623 23567.
Manager: George Foster.
Ground capacity: 10,468.
Record attendance: 24,467 v Nottingham Forest, FA Cup Third Round, 10th January, 1953.
Record victory: 8–0 v Scarborough, FA Cup First Round, 22nd November, 1952.
Record defeat: 1–8 v Walsall, Third Division (North), 19th January, 1933.
Record transfer received: £500,000 from Middlesbrough for Simon Coleman, September 1989.
Record transfer paid: £80,000 to Leicester City for Steve Wilkinson, September 1989.
Honours: *Third Division Champions*: 1976–77.
Fourth Division Champions: 1974–75.
Freight Rover Trophy winners: 1986–87.
Football League record: 1931 elected to Third Division (South); 1932–37 Third Division (North); 1937–47 Third Division (South); 1947–58 Third Division (North);

1958–60 Third Division; 1960–63 Fourth Division;
1963–72 Third Division; 1972–75 Fourth Division; 1975–77
Third Division; 1977–78 Second Division; 1978–80 Third
Division; 1980–86 Fourth Division; 1986–91 Third
Division; 1991– Fourth Division.

Managers since the War: Roy Goodall 1945–49; Freddie
Steele 1949–51; George Jobey 1952–53; Stan Mercer
1953–55; Charlie Mitten 1956–58; Sam Weaver 1958–60;
Raich Carter 1960–63; Tommy Cummings 1963–67;
Tommy Eggleston 1967–70; Jock Basford 1970–71; Danny
Williams 1971–74; Dave Smith 1974–76; Peter Morris
1976–78; Billy Bingham 1978–79; Mick Jones 1979–81;
Stuart Boam 1981–83; Ian Greaves 1983–89; George Foster
1989– .

Some former famous players: Harry Johnson; Ted
Harston; John McClelland; Rod Arnold.

Formed in 1910 when Mansfield Wesleyans decided to
change their name to Mansfield Town and join the new
Central Alliance League.

   Town were elected to the Third Division (South) in 1931
and defeated Swindon Town 3–2 at home in their first
League game.

MANCHESTER UNITED
Formed: 1878 as Newton Heath.
1902 as Manchester United. Turned
professional: 1885.
Nickname: Red Devils.
Address: Old Trafford, Manchester,
M16 0RA.
Telephone: 061 872 1661.
Manager: Alex Ferguson.
Ground capacity: 50,726.
Record attendance: (for club game)
70,504 v Aston Villa, First Division,
27th December, 1920; (ground)
76,962 Wolverhampton Wanderers v
Grimsby Town, FA Cup Semi-Final,
25th March, 1939.

Record victory: 10–0 v RSC Anderlecht, European Cup
Preliminary Round (second leg), 26th September, 1956.
Record defeat: 0–7 v Blackburn Rovers, First
Division, 10th April,
1926 and v Wolverhampton Wanderers, Second Division,
26th December, 1931.
Record transfer received: £1,800,000 from Barcelona for
Mark Hughes, August 1986.

Record transfer paid: £2,300,000 to Middlesbrough for Gary Pallister, August 1989.
Honours: League Champions: 1907–08; 1910–11; 1951–52; 1955–56; 1956–57; 1964–65; 1966–67.
Second Division Champions: 1935–36; 1974–75.
FA Cup Winners: 1909; 1948; 1963; 1977; 1983; 1985; 1990. *European Cup Winners' Cup Winners*: 1990–91.
European Cup Winners: 1967–68.
Football League record: 1892 elected to First Division; 1894–1906 Second Division; 1906–22 First Division; 1922–25 Second Division; 1925–31 First Division; 1931–36 Second Division; 1936–37 First Division; 1937–38 Second Division; 1938–74 First Division; 1974–75 Second Division; 1975– First Division.
Managers since the War: Matt Busby 1945–69; Wilf McGuinness 1969–70; Frank O'Farrell 1971–72; Tommy Docherty 1972–77; Dave Sexton 1977–81; Ron Atkinson 1981–86; Alex Ferguson 1986– .
Some former famous players: Dennis Viollet; Ray Woods; Tommy Taylor; Duncan Edwards; Roger Byrne; Bill Foulkes; Bobby Charlton; George Best; Steve Coppell.

Formed in 1878 by employees of the Lancashire and Yorkshire Railway Company as Newton Heath Cricket and Football Club.

Elected to the First Division in 1892, Newton Heath lost their first League game 4–3 at Blackburn Rovers.

When Newton Heath went bankrupt in 1902 a new club, Manchester United, was born.

MIDDLESBROUGH

Formed: 1877. Turned professional: 1889; amateur in 1892 and reverted to professional 1899.
Nickname: The Boro.
Address: Ayresome Park, Middlesbrough, Cleveland. TS1 4PB.
Telephone: 0642 819659. ClubCall: 0898 121181.
Manager: Lennie Lawrence.
Ground capacity: 30,000.
Record attendance: 53,596 v Newcastle United, First Division, 27th December, 1979.
Record victory: 9–0 v Brighton & Hove Albion, Second Division, 23rd August, 1958.

Record defeat: 0–9 v Blackburn Rovers, Second Division, 6th November, 1954.
Record transfer received: £2,300,000 from Manchester United for Gary Pallister, August 1989.
Record transfer paid: £700,000 to Manchester United for Peter Davenport, November 1988.
Honours: *Second Division Champions*: 1926–27; 1928–29; 1973–74.
FA Amateur Cup Winners: 1895; 1898.
AngloScottish Cup Winners: 1975–76.
Football League record: 1899 elected to Second Division; 1902–24 First Division; 1924–27 Second Division; 1927–28 First Division; 1928–29 Second Division; 1929–54 First Division; 1954–66 Second Division; 1966–67 Third Division; 1967–74 Second Division; 1974–82 First Division; 1982–86 Second Division; 1986–87 Third Division; 1987–88 Second Division; 1988–89 First Division; 1989– Second Division.
Managers since the War: David Jack 1944–52; Walter Rowley 1952–54; Bob Dennison 1954–63; Raich Carter 1963–66; Stan Anderson 1966–73; Jack Charlton 1973–77; John Neal 1977–81; Bobby Murdoch 1981–82; Malcolm Allison 1982–84; Willie Maddren 1984–86; Bruce Rioch 1986–90; Colin Todd 1990–91; Lennie Lawrence 1991– .
Some former famous players: Tim Williamson; George Camsell; Wilf Mannion; Brian Clough; Alan Peacock.

Formed in 1877 after a meeting in the town's Talbot Hotel.
   They turned professional in 1889, but reverted to amateurism three years later.
   The club won the Amateur Cup twice and then became professional again in 1899, the year they were elected to the Second Division.
   Boro lost their first League game 3–0 away at Lincoln City.

MILLWALL

Formed: 1885. Turned professional: 1893.
Nickname: The Lions.
Address: The Den, Cold Blow Lane, London, SE14 5RH.
Telephone: 071 639 3143. ClubCall: 0898 121143.
Manager: Bruce Rioch.
Ground capacity: 26,000.
Record attendance: 48,672 v Derby County, FA Cup Fifth Round, 20th February, 1937.
Record victory: 9-1 v Torquay United, Third Division (South), 29th August, 1927.
Record defeat: 1-9 v Aston Villa, FA Cup Fourth Round, 28th January, 1946.
Record transfer received: £1,500,000 from Aston Villa for Tony Cascarino, March 1990.
Record transfer paid: £800,000 to Derby County for Paul Goddard, December, 1989.
Honours: *Second Division Champions*: 1987-88.
Third Division (South) Champions: 1927-28; 1937-38.
Fourth Division Champions: 1961-62.
Football League Trophy Winners: 1982-83.
Football League record: 1920 original members of Third Division; 1921 Third Division (South); 1928-34 Second Division; 1934-38 Third Division (South); 1938-48 Second Division; 1948-58 Third Division (South); 1958-62 Fourth Division; 1962-64 Third Division; 1964-65 Fourth Division; 1965-66 Third Division; 1966-75 Second Division; 1975-76 Third Division; 1976-79 Second Division; 1979-85 Third Division; 1985-88 Second Division; 1988-90 First Division; 1990- Second Division.
Managers since the War: Jack Cock 1944-48; Charlie Hewitt 1948-56; Ron Gray 1956-57; Jimmy Seed 1958-59; Reg Smith 1959-61; Ron Gray 1961-63; Billy Gray 1963-66; Benny Fenton 1966-74; Gordon Jago 1974-77; George Petchey 1978-80; Peter Anderson 1980-82; George Graham 1982-86; John Docherty 1986-90; Bob Pearson 1990; Bruce Rioch 1990 - .
Some former famous players: Richard Parker; Derek Possee; Eamonn Dunphy; Barry Kitchener; Tony Cascarino.

Formed in 1885 by workers at a jam factory in West Ferry Road. They called the new club Millwall Rovers and had their headquarters in the Islanders pub in Tooke Street, Millwall.

In 1886 their home ground was called Back of the Lord Nelson.

Three years later the name of the club was changed to Millwall Athletic.

But they were elected as founder members of the Third Division as Millwall in 1920. The club kicked off their League career with a 2-0 victory over Bristol Rovers at The Den.

NEWCASTLE UNITED

Formed: 1881. Turned professional: 1889.
Nickname: The Magpies.
Address: St. James' Park, Newcastle-upon-Tyne. NE1 4ST.
Telephone: 091 232 8361. ClubCall: 0898 121190.
Manager: Ossie Ardiles.
Ground capacity: 37,637.
Record attendance: 68,386 v Chelsea, First Division, 3rd September, 1930.
Record victory: 13-0 v Newport County, Second Division, 5th October, 1946.
Record defeat: 0-9 v Burton Wanderers, Second Division, 15th April, 1895.
Record transfer received: £2,000,000 from Tottenham Hotspur for Paul Gascoigne, July 1988.
Record transfer paid: £850,000 to Wimbledon for Dave Beasant, June 1988 and 850,000 to Wimbledon for Andy Thorn, August 1988.
Honours: *League Champions*: 1904-05; 1906-07; 1908-09; 1926-27.
Second Division Champions: 1964-65.
FA Cup Winners: 1910; 1924; 1932; 1951; 1952; 1955.
Texaco Cup Winners: 1973-74; 1974-75.
European Fairs Cup (now UEFA Cup) Winners: 1968-69.
Anglo/Italian Cup Winners: 1973.
Football League record: 1893 elected to Second Division; 1893-1934 First Division; 1934-48 Second Division; 1948-61 First Division; 1961-65 Second Division; 1965-78 First Division; 1978-84 Second Division; 1984-89 First Division; 1989- Second Division.
Managers since the War: George Martin 1947-50; Stan

Seymour 1950–54; Duggie Livingstone 1954–56; Stan
Seymour 1956–58; Charlie Mitten 1958–61; Norman Smith
1961–62; Joe Harvey 1962–75; Gordon Lee 1975–77;
Richard Dinnis 1977; Bill McGarry 1977–80; Arthur Cox
1980–84; Jack Charlton 1984; Willie McFaul 1985–88; Jim
Smith 1988–91; Ossie Ardiles 1991– .
Some former famous players: Hughie Gallacher; Jackie
Milburn; Joe Harvey; Alf McMichael; Peter Beardsley;
Chris Waddle; Kevin Keegan; Malcolm Macdonald; Paul
Gascoigne.

Called Stanley FC when formed in 1881. A year later the
club changed their name to Newcastle East End because
they were constantly being confused with another club
called Stanley situated in neighbouring Co.Durham.
　A few months later another club Newcastle West End
were formed. When they became defunct in 1889, the East
End club were offered the use of their St.James' Park
ground.
　The proposal was accepted and at a meeting in 1892 the
club changed their name to Newcastle United.
　A year later they were elected to the Second Division of
the Football League.
　Newcastle's first League game away at Royal Arsenal
ended in a 2–2 draw.

NORTHAMPTON TOWN

Formed: 1897. Turned professional:
1901.
Nickname: The Cobblers.
Address: County Ground,
Abingdon Avenue, Northampton.
NN1 4PS.
Telephone: 0604 234100.
Manager: Theo Foley.
Ground capacity: 11,907.
Record attendance: 24,523 v
Fulham, First Division, 23rd April,
1966.
Record victory: 10–0 v Walsall,
Third Division (South), 5th
November, 1927.
Record defeat: 0–11 v Southampton, Southern League,
28th December, 1901.
Record transfer received: £265,000 from Watford for
Richard Hill, July 1987.

Record transfer paid: £85,000 to Manchester City for
Tony Adcock, January 1988.
Honours: *Third Division Champions*: 1962–63.
Fourth Division Champions: 1986–87.
Football League record: 1920 original member of Third
Division; 1921 Third Division (South); 1958–61 Fourth
Division; 1961–63 Third Division; 1963–65 Second
Division; 1965–66 First Division; 1966–67 Second
Division; 1967–69 Third Division; 1969–76 Fourth
Division; 1976–77 Third Division; 1977–78 Fourth
Division; 1987–90 Third Division; 1990– Fourth Division.
Managers since the War: Bob Dennison 1949–54; Dave
Smith 1954–59; Dave Bowen 1959–67; Tony Marchi
1967–68; Ron Flowers 1968–69; Dave Bowen 1969–72; Jim
Baxter 1972–73; Bill Dodgin jnr 1973–76; Pat Crerand
1976–77; Bill Dodgin jnr 1977; John Petts 1977–78; Mike
Keen 1978–79; Clive Walker 1979–80; Bill Dodgin jnr
1980–82; Clive Walker 1982–84; Tony Barton 1984–85;
Graham Carr 1985–90; Theo Foley 1990– .
Some former famous players: Jack English; Cliff Holton;
Tommy Fowler.

Formed in 1897 by local school teachers and immediately
shared the same pitch with Northamptonshire Cricket
Club. They still play at the County Ground and are now
the only club in the Football League to play at a three-
sided stadium.

Town joined the Third Division of the Football League
in 1920, losing their first game 2–0 away at Grimsby Town.

During a sensational spell in the 1960's Town climbed to
the First Division. By the end of the decade they had
slumped back to the Fourth Division.

NORWICH CITY
Formed: 1902. Turned professional: 1905.
Nickname: The Canaries.
Address: Carrow Road, Norwich. NR1 1JE.
Telephone: 0603 612131. ClubCall: 0898 121144.
Manager: Dave Stringer.
Ground capacity: 24,284.
Record attendance: 43,984 v Leicester City, FA Cup Sixth Round, 30th March, 1963.
Record victory: 10–2 v Coventry City, Third Division (South), 15th March, 1930.
Record defeat: 2–10 v Swindon Town, Southern League, 5th September, 1908.
Record transfer received: £1,250,000 from Arsenal for Andy Linighan, July 1990.
Record transfer paid: £1,000,000 to Port Vale for Darren Beckford, June 1991.
Honours: *Second Division Champions*: 1971–72; 1985–86.
Third Division (South) Champions: 1933–34.
Football League Cup Winners: 1962; 1985.
Football League record: 1920 original member Third Division; 1921 Third Division (South); 1934–39 Second Division; 1946–58 Third Division (South); 1958–60 Third Division; 1960–72 Second Division; 1972–74 First Division; 1974–75 Second Division; 1975–81 First Division; 1981–82 Second Division; 1982–85 First Division; 1985–86 Second Division; 1986– First Division.
Managers since the War: Duggie Lochhead 1945–50; Norman Low 1950–55; Tom Parker 1955–57; Archie Macaulay 1957–61; Willie Reid 1961–62; George Swindin 1962; Ron Ashman 1962–66; Lol Morgan 1966–69; Ron Saunders 1969–73; John Bond 1973–80; Ken Brown 1980–87; Dave Stringer 1987– .
Some former famous players: Ron Ashman; Johnny Galvin; Ralph Hunt; Martin O'Neill; Michael Phelan; Chris Woods; Dave Watson; Andy Linighan; Andy Townsend; Mick Channon; Martin Peters.

Formed by local school teachers, records show that the club's first game was on a ground on the Newmarket Road in 1902.

They moved to a disused chalk pit called The Nest six

years later ... an apt name for The Canaries.

City were elected to the Third Division in 1920. Their first League game, at Plymouth Argyle, ended in a 1–1 draw.

In 1935 the FA told Norwich that The Nest was too small for League football. So the club moved half-a-mile along the River Wensum to their present Carrow Road stadium.

NOTTINGHAM FOREST

Formed: 1865. Turned professional: 1889.

Nickname: The Reds.

Address: City Ground, Nottingham. NG2 5FJ.

Telephone: 0602 822202. ClubCall: 0898 121174.

Manager: Brian Clough.

Ground capacity: 31,920 (15,114 seats).

Record attendance: 49,945 v Manchester United, First Division, 28th October, 1967.

Record victory: 14–0 v Clapton, FA Cup First Round, 17th January, 1891.

Record defeat: 1–9 v Blackburn Rovers, Second Division, 10th April, 1937.

Record transfer received: £1,500,000 from Manchester United for Neil Webb, August 1989.

Record transfer paid: £1,250,000 to Coventry City for Ian Wallace, July 1980.

Honours: *League Champions*: 1977–78.

Second Division Champions: 1906–07; 1921–22.

Third Division (South) Champions: 1950–51.

FA Cup Winners: 1898; 1959.

Anglo/Scottish Cup Winners: 1976–77.

Football League Cup Winners: 1977–78; 1978–79; 1988–89; 1989–90.

Simod Cup Winners: 1989.

European Cup Winners: 1978–79; 1979–80.

Super Cup Winners: 1979–80.

Football League record: 1892 elected to First Division; 1906–07 Second Division; 1907–11 First Division; 1911–22 Second Division; 1922–25 First Division; 1925–49 Second Division; 1949–51 Third Division (South); 1951–57 Second Division; 1957–72 First Division; 1972–77 Second Division; 1977– First Division.

Managers since the War: Billy Walker 1939–60; Andy

Beattie 1960–63; Johnny Carey 1963–68; Matt Gillies 1969–72; Dave Mackay 1972; Allan Brown 1973–75; Brian Clough 1975– .
Some former famous players: Grenville Morris; Wally Ardron; Bob McKinlay; Martin O'Neill; Trevor Francis; John Robertson; Peter Shilton; Peter Davenport; Larry Lloyd; Tony Woodcock; Archie Gemmill; Frank Gray.

The third oldest club in the Football League was called the Forest FC when first formed in 1865 by members of a local shinny club. Shinny was a variation of hockey played in the North.

A referee's whistle was used for the first time in a game between Forest and Sheffield Norfolk in 1878.

The club played on six different home grounds, including Trent Bridge, before moving to the City Ground in 1898.

By then Forest had already joined the Football League. They drew their first game in September 1892, 2–2 away at Everton.

NOTTS COUNTY

Formed: 1862. Turned professional: 1885.
Nickname: The Magpies.
Address: County Ground, Meadow Lane, Nottingham. NG2 3HJ.
Telephone: 0602 861155. ClubCall: 0898 121101.
Manager: Neil Warnock.
Ground capacity: 21,097.
Record attendance: 47,310 v York City, FA Cup Sixth Round, 12th March, 1955.
Record victory: 15–0 v Rotherham Town, FA Cup First Round, 24th October, 1885.
Record defeat: 1–9 v Blackburn Rovers, First Division, 16th November, 1889 and v Aston Villa, First Division, 29th September, 1888 and v Portsmouth, Second Division, 9th April, 1927.
Record transfer received: £350,000 from Tottenham Hotspur for John Chiedozie, August 1984.
Record transfer paid: £600,000 to Orient for John Chiedozie, August 1981.
Honours: *Second Division Champions*: 1896–97; 1913–14; 1922–23.

Third Division (South) Champions: 1930–31; 1949–50.
Fourth Division Champions: 1970–71.
FA Cup Winners: 1893–94.
Football League record: 1888 founder member of
Football League; 1893–97 Second Division; 1897–1913
First Division; 1913–14 Second Division; 1914–20 First
Division; 1920–23 Second Division; 1923–26 First
Division; 1926–30 Second Division; 1930–31 Third
Division (South); 1931–35 Second Division; 1935–50 Third
Division (South); 1950–58 Second Division; 1958–59 Third
Division; 1959–60 Fourth Division; 1960–64 Third
Division; 1964–71 Fourth Division; 1971–73 Third
Division; 1973–81 Second Division; 1981–84 First Division;
1984–85 Second Division; 1985–90 Third Division;
1990–91 Second Division; 1991– First Division.
Managers since the War: Arthur Stollery 1946–49; Eric
Houghton 1949–53; George Poyser 1953–57; Tommy
Lawton 1957–58; Frank Hill 1958–61; Tim Coleman
1961–63; Eddie Lowe 1963–65; Tim Coleman 1965–66;
Jack Burkitt 1966–67; Andy Beattie 1967; Billy Gray
1967–68; Jimmy Sirrel 1969–75; Ron Fenton 1975–77;
Jimmy Sirrel 1978–82; Howard Wilkinson 1982–83; Larry
Lloyd 1983–84; Richie Barker 1984–85; Jimmy Sirrel
1985–87; John Barnwell 1987–88; Neil Warnock 1989– .
Some former famous players: Albert Ironmonger; Tom
Keetley; Harry Cursham; Tommy Lawton; Les Bradd;
Martin O'Neill.

The oldest club in the Football League was formed in 1862,
although they only played friendly games for the first year
or so of their existence.

Notts FC didn't really start to function until 1864 after a
meeting was held in the George 1V Hotel.

The club became founder members of the Football
League in 1888. Notts lost their first game 2–1 away at
Everton.

OLDHAM ATHLETIC
Formed: 1895. Turned professional: 1899.
Nickname: The Latics.
Address: Boundary Park, Oldham.
Telephone: 061 624 4972. ClubCall: 0898 121142.
Manager: Joe Royle.
Ground capacity: 19,432.
Record attendance: 47,671 v Sheffield Wednesday, FA Cup Fourth Round, 25th January, 1930.
Record victory: 11–0 v Southport, Fourth Division, 26th December, 1962.
Record defeat: 4–13 v Tranmere Rovers, Third Division (North), 26th December, 1935.
Record transfer received: £1,000,000 from Everton for Mike Milligan, August 1990.
Record transfer paid: £460,000 to Hull City for Richard Jobson, August 1990.
Honours: *Second Division Champions*: 1990–1; *Third Division (North) Champions*: 1952–53.
Third Division Champions: 1973–74.
Football League record: 1907 elected to Second Division; 1910–23 First Division; 1923–35 Second Division; 1935–53 Third Division (North); 1953–54 Second Division; 1954–58 Third Division (North); 1958–63 Fourth Division; 1963–69 Third Division; 1969–71 Fourth Division; 1971–74 Third Division; 1974–91 Second Division; 1991– First Division.
Managers since the War: Billy Wootton 1947–50; George Hardwick 1950–56; Ted Goodier 1956–58; Norman Dodgin 1958–60; Jack Rowley 1960–63; Les McDowell 1963–65; Gordon Hurst 1965–66; Jimmy McIlroy 1966–68; Jack Rowley 1968–69; Jimmy Frizzell 1970–82; Joe Royle 1982– .
Some former famous players: Albert Gray; Tom Davis; Andy Linighan; Andy Goram; Mike Milligan; Ian Wood.

In 1895 the landlord of the Featherstall and Junction Hotel formed a football team called Pine Villa.

Four years later when another local club Oldham County went into liquidation Pine Villa took over their Sheepfoot Lane ground. A few weeks later they changed their name to Oldham Athletic.

The club joined the Second Division in 1907 and won their first League game 3–1 away at Stoke City.

OXFORD UNITED
Formed: 1893. Turned professional: 1949.
Nickname: The U's.
Address: Manor Ground, Headington, Oxford.
Telephone: 0865 61503. ClubCall: 0898 121172.
Manager: Brian Horton.
Ground capacity: 11,117.
Record attendance: 22,750 v Preston North End, FA Cup Sixth Round, 29th February, 1964.
Record victory: 7–0 v Barrow, Fourth Division, 19th December, 1964.
Record defeat: 0–6 v Liverpool, Second Division, 22nd March, 1986.
Record transfer received: £1,000,000 from Derby County for Dean Saunders, October 1988.
Record transfer paid: £275,000 to Swansea City for Andy Melville, July 1990.
Honours: *Second Division Champions*: 1984–85.
Third Division Champions: 1967–68; 1983–84.
Football League Cup Winners: 1985–86.
Football League record: 1962 elected to Fourth Division; 1965–68 Third Division; 1968–76 Second Division; 1976–84 Third Division; 1984–85 Second Division; 1985–88 First Division; 1988– Second Division.
Managers since the War: Harry Thompson 1949–58; Arthur Turner 1959–69; Ron Saunders 1969; George Summers 1969–75; Mike Brown 1975–79; Bill Asprey 1979–80; Ian Greaves 1980–82; Jim Smith 1982–85; Maurice Evans 1985–88; Mark Lawrenson 1988; Brian Horton 1988– .
Some former famous players: Graham Atkinson; John Shuker; John Aldridge; Ray Houghton; Neil Slatter; Dean Saunders.

Formed in 1893 as Headington, they added United three years later and played on a pitch behind the Britannia Inn.

The club didn't join the Football League until many years later, but they do deserve a very important place in soccer history.

In December 1950 Southern Leaguers Headington became Britain's first professional club to install floodlighting. They were temporary lights borrowed from Oxford University and mounted on poles. But they were the first and proved good enough to allow a friendly with Banbury to be played to raise money for local hospitals.

The club changed their name to Oxford United in 1960 and won the Southern League title in 1961 and 1962 before replacing Accrington Stanley in the Football League.

Oxford's first game in the Fourth Division was away at Barrow in August, 1962. They lost 3–2, but were to more that avenge that thrashing two years later when they achieved their record victory to date.

PETERBOROUGH UNITED
Formed: 1934. Turned professional: 1934.
Nickname: The Posh.
Address: London Road Ground, Peterborough, PE2 8AL.
Telephone: 0733 63947. ClubCall: 0898 121654.
Manager: David Booth.
Ground capacity: 28,000.
Record attendance: 30,096 v Swansea Town, FA Cup Fifth Round, 20th February, 1965.
Record victory: 8–1 v Oldham Athletic, Fourth Division, 26th November, 1969.
Record defeat: 1–8 v Northampton Town, FA Cup Second Round replay, 18th December, 1946.
Record transfer received: £110,000 from Blackpool for Bob Doyle, July 1979.
Record transfer paid: £100,000 to Halifax Town for David Robinson, July 1989.
Honours: *Fourth Division Champions*: 1960–61; 1973–74.
Football League record: 1960 elected to Fourth Division; 1961–68
Third Division: demoted for financial irregularities; 1968–74 Fourth Division; 1974–79 Third Division; 1979–91 Fourth Division; 1991– Third Division.
Managers since the War: Jack Blood 1948–50; Bob Gurney 1950–52; Jack Fairbrother 1952–54; George Swindon 1954–58; Jimmy Hagan 1958–62; Jack Fairbrother 1962–64; Gordon Clark 1964–67; Norman Rigby 1967–69; Jim Iley 1969–72; Noel Cantwell 1972–77; John Barnwell 1977–78; Billy Hails 1978–79; Peter Morris 1979–82; Martin Wilkinson 1982–83; John Wile 1983–86; Noel Cantwell 1986–88; Mick Jones 1988–89; Mark

Lawrenson 1989–90; David Booth 1990– .
Some former famous players: Terry Bly; Jim Hall; Tony
Millington; Tommy Robson; John Wile.

Formed in 1934 and for years were a comparatively
unknown Midland League club until a sensational run in
the 1950's made national headlines.

Between 1955–60 they lost just one game out of 103
played on their London Road home ground, scoring 428
goals.

Arsenal were the vistors when the club installed
floodlights in 1957. More improvements were made to the
ground where gates regularly topped the 10,000 mark.

Election to the Football League was finally achieved in
1960 when they replaced Gateshead.

Peterborough won their first League game 3–0 at home
to Wrexham and ended the season as Champions of the
Fourth Division.

PLYMOUTH ARGYLE

Formed: 1886. Turned professional:
1903.
Nickname: The Pilgrims.
Address: Home Park, Plymouth,
Devon, PL2 3DQ.
Telephone: 0752 562561. ClubCall:
0898 121688.
Manager: David Kemp.
Ground capacity: 26,000.
Record attendance: 43,596 v Aston
Villa, Second Division, 10th
October, 1936.
Record victory: 8–1 v Millwall,
Second Division, 16th January, 1932.
Record defeat: 0–9 v Stoke City, 17th December, 1960.
Record transfer received: £250,000 from Everton for
Gary Megson, February 1980.
Record transfer paid: £170,000 to Sheffield Wednesday for
Mark Smith, January 1987.
Honours: *Third Division (South) Champions*: 1929–30;
1951–52.
Third Division Champions: 1958–59.
Football League record: 1920 original member of Third
Division; 1921–30 Third Division (South); 1930–50 Second
Division; 1950–52 Third Division (South); 1952–56 Second
Division; 1956–58 Third Division (South); 1958–59 Third
Division; 1959–68 Second Division; 1968–75 Third

Division; 1975–77 Second Division; 1977–86 Third
Division; 1986– Second Division.
Managers since the War: Jimmy Rae 1948–55; Jack
Rowley 1955–60; Neil Dougall 1961; Ellis Stuttard
1961–63; Andy Beattie 1963–64; Malcolm Allison 1964–65;
Derek Ufton 1965–68; Billy Bingham 1968–70; Ellis
Stuttard 1970–72; Tony Waiters 1972–77; Mike Kelly
1977–78; Malcolm Allison 1978–79; Bobby Saxton
1979–81; Bobby Moncur 1981–83; Johnny Hore 1983–84;
Dave Smith 1984–88; Ken Brown 1988–90; David Kemp
1990– .
Some former famous players: Jack Cock; Moses Russell;
Sammy Black; Kevin Hodges; Norman Piper; Paul
Mariner.

Formed as Argyle Athletic in 1886 after a meeting held in
Argyle Terrace, Mutley. The club played cricket, soccer
and rugby. Rugby was the most popular sport in the area
at the time.
   In 1903 due to the growing interest in football, mainly
by members of the armed forces, cricket and rugby were
dropped and the club was renamed Plymouth Argyle.
   They became founder members of the Third Division in
1920 and drew their first League match 1–1 at home to
Norwich City.

PORTSMOUTH

Formed and Turned Professional:
1898.
Nickname: Pompey.
Address: Fratton Park, Frogmore
Road, Portsmouth, PO4 8RA.
Telephone: 0705 731204. ClubCall:
0898 121182.
Manager: Jim Smith.
Ground capacity: 28,000.
Record attendance: 51,385 v Derby
County, FA Cup Sixth Round, 26th
February, 1949.
Record victory: 9–1 v Notts County,
Second Division, 9th April, 1927.
Record defeat: 0–10 v Leicester City, First Division, 20th
October, 1928.
Record transfer received: £915,000 from AC Milan for
Mark Hateley, June 1984.
Record transfer paid: £450,000 to QPR for Colin Clarke,
May 1990.

Honours: *First Division Champions*: 1948–49; 1949–50.
Third Division (South) Champions: 1923–24.
Third Division Champions: 1961–62; 1982–83.
FA Cup Winners: 1939.
Football League record: 1920 original member Third
Division; 1921 Third Division (South); 1924–27 Second
Division; 1927–59 First Division; 1959–61 Second
Division; 1961–62 Third Division; 1962–76 Second
Division; 1976–78 Third Division; 1978–80 Fourth
Division; 1980–83 Third Division; 1983–87 Second
Division; 1987–88 First Division; 1988– Second Division.

Managers since the War: Bob Jackson 1947–52; Eddie
Lever 1952–58; Freddie Cox 1958–61; George Smith
1961–70; Ron Tindall 1970–73; John Mortimore 1973–74;
Ian St. John 1974–77; Jimmy Dickinson 1977–79; Frank
Burrows 1979–82; Bobby Campbell 1982–84; Alan Ball
1984–89; John Gregory 1989–90; Frank Burrows 1990–91;
Jim Smith 1991.

Some former famous players: Billy Haines; Jimmy
Dickinson; Jimmy Scoular; Peter Harris; Mark Hateley.

When the Royal Artillery club was suspended by the FA
for breaking amateur regulations, local businessmen
decided to form a new professional club.

They raised £4,950 and bought some ground close to
Fratton railway station and applied to join the Southern
League.

So Portsmouth were launched in 1899 and had won their
first Southern League title by 1902.

They became one of the founder members of the Third
Division in 1920 and won their first game 3–0 at home to
Swansea Town.

PORT VALE
Formed: 1876. Turned professional: 1885.
Nickname: The Valiants.
Address: Vale Park, Burslem, Stoke-on-Trent.
Telephone: 0708 814134. ClubCall: 0898 121636.
Manager: John Rudge.
Ground capacity: 20,950.
Record attendance: 50,000 v Aston Villa, FA Cup Fifth Round, 20th February, 1960.
Record victory: 9–1 v Chesterfield, Second Division, 24th September, 1932.
Record defeat: 0–10 v Sheffield United, Second Division, 10th December, 1892 and v Notts County, Second Division, 26th February, 1895.
Record transfer received: £300,000 from Charlton Athletic for Andy Jones, September 1987.
Record transfer paid: £200,000 to Middlesbrough for Dean Glover, February 1989 and to Leeds United for Neil Aspin, July 1989.
Honours: *Third Division (North) Champions*: 1929–30; 1953–54.
Fourth Division Champions: 1958–59.
Football League record: original member Second Division 1892–96; Failed re-election 1896; Re-elected 1898; Resigned 1907; Returned October 1919 when they took over Leeds City fixtures; 1929–30 Third Division (North); 1930–36 Second Division; 1936–38 Third Division (North); 1938–52 Third Division (South); 1952–54 Third Division (North); 1954–57 Second Division; 1957–58 Third Division (South); 1958–59 Fourth Division; 1959–5 Third Division; 1965–70 Fourth Division; 1970–78 Third Division; 1978–83 Fourth Division; 1983–84 Third Division; 1984–86 Fourth Division; 1986–89 Third Division; 1989– Second Division.
Managers since the War: Gordon Hodgson 1946–51; Ivor Powell 1951; Freddie Steele 1951–57; Norman Low 1957–62; Freddie Steele 1962–65; Jackie Mudie 1965–67; Sir Stanley Matthews 1965–68; Gordon Lee 1968–74; Roy Sproson 1974–77; Colin Harper 1977; Bobby Smith 1977–78; Dennis Butler 1978–79; Alan Bloor 1979; John McGrath 1980–83; John Rudge 1983– .
Some former famous players: Wilf Kirkham; Sammy Morgan; Roy Sproson.

Formed in 1876 at a meeting in a house of the same name in Burslem, one of the six towns of the Potteries. Port Vale dropped Burslem from their name when the club moved to a new home in Hanley in 1913.

The club were already a member of the Football League, having been elected to the newly formed Second Division in 1892.

Vale were beaten 5-1 away at Small Heath in their first League game.

PRESTON NORTH END

Formed: 1881. Turned professional: 1885.

Nickname: The Lilywhites or North End.

Address: Deepdale, Preston. PR1 6RU.

Telephone: 0772 795919.

ClubCall: 0898 121173.

Manager: Les Chapman.

Ground capacity: 17,000.

Record attendance: 42,684 v Arsenal, First Division, 23rd April, 1938.

Record victory: 26-0 v Hyde, FA Cup First Round, 15th October, 1887.

Record defeat: 0-7 v Blackpool, First Division, 1st May, 1948.

Record transfer received: £65,000 from Manchester City for Michael Robinson, June 1979.

Record transfer paid: £125,000 to Norwich City for Mike Flynn, December 1989.

Honours: *League Champions*: 1888-89; (first ever League Champions); 1889-90.

Second Division Champions: 1903-04; 1912-13; 1950-51.

Third Division Champions: 1970-71.

FA Cup Winners: 1889; 1938.

Double Performed: 1888-89.

Football League record: 1888 founder member of Football League; 1901-04 Second Division; 1904-12 First Division; 1912-13 Second Division; 1913-14 First Division; 1914-15 Second Division; 1919-25 First Division; 1925-34 Second Division; 1934-49 First Division; 1949-51 Second Division; 1951-61 First Division; 1961-70 Second Division; 1970-71 Third Division; 1971-74 Second Division; 1974-78 Third Division; 1978-81 Second Division; 1981-85 Third Division; 1985-87 Fourth Division; 1987- Third Division.

Managers since the War: Will Scott 1949–53; Scot Symon 1953–54; Frank Hill 1954–56; Cliff Britton 1956–61; Jimmy Milne 1961–68; Bobby Seith 1968–70; Alan Ball Snr 1970–73; Bobby Charlton 1973–75; Harry Catterick 1975–77; Nobby Stiles 1977–81; Tommy Docherty 1981; Gordon Lee 1981–83; Alan Kelly 1983–85; Tommy Booth 1985–86; Brian Kidd 1986; John McGrath 1986–90; Les Chapman 1990– .

Some former famous players: Ted Harper; Tom Finney; Alan Kelly; Tommy Docherty; Bill Shankly; Michael Robinson.

Formed in 1881 when the North End Cricket and Rugby Club decided to convert to football.

Although beaten 16–0 by Blackburn Rovers in a friendly at Deepdale in their first game, the club made a successful application to join the Lancashire FA.

Seven years later Preston became one of the twelve founder members of the Football League. They defeated Burnley 5–2 in their first match.

Proud Preston became the first League club to win the Championship and perform the Double when they captured the title and FA Cup in that first season.

QUEENS PARK RANGERS

Formed: 1886. Turned professional: 1898.

Nickname: Rangers or R's.

Address: South Africa Road, London, W12 7PA.

Telephone: 081 743 0262. ClubCall: 0898 121173.

Manager: Gerry Francis.

Ground capacity: 23,480 (23,000 covered).

Record attendance: 35,353 v Leeds United, First Division, 27th April, 1974.

Record victory: 9–2 v Tranmere Rovers, Third Division, 3rd December, 1960.

Record defeat: 1–8 v Mansfield Town, Third Division, 15th March, 1965 and v Manchester United, First Division, 19th March, 1969.

Record transfer received: £1,300,000 from Arsenal for David Seaman, May 1990.

Record transfer paid: £1,000,000 to Luton Town for Roy Wegerle, December 1989.

Honours: *Second Division Champions*: 1982–83.
Third Division (South) Champions: 1947–48.
Third Division Champions: 1966–67.
Football League Cup Winners: 1966–67.
Football League record: 1920 original member of Third
Division; 1921 Third Division (South); 1948–52 Second
Division; 1952–58 Third Division (South); 1958–67 Third
Division; 1967–68 Second Division; 1968–69 First
Division; 1969–73 Second Division; 1973–79 First
Division; 1979–83 Second Division; 1983– First Division.
Managers since the War: Dave Mangnall 1944–52; Jack
Taylor 1952–59; Alec Stock 1959–65; Jimmy Andrews
1965; Bill Dodgin Jnr 1968; Tommy Docherty 1968; Les
Allen 1969–70; Gordon Jago 1971–74; Dave Sexton
1974–77; Frank Sibley 1977–78; Steve Burtenshaw
1978–79; Tommy Docherty 1979–80; Terry Venables
1980–84; Gordon Jago 1984; Alan Mullery 1984; Frank
Sibley 1984–85; Jim Smith 1985–88; Trevor Francis
1988–90; Don Howe 1990–91; Gerry Francis 1991– .
Some former famous players: George Goddard; Don
Givens; Tony Ingham; Mark Lazarus; Mike Keen; Terry
Fenwick; Trevor Francis; Stan Bowles; Rodney Marsh;
Gerry Francis; Clive Allen.

Formed in 1886 when Christchurch Rangers amalgamated
with St. Jude's Institute FC.
    As most of the players lived in the Queens Park district
of West London this name was soon adopted by the club.
    Founder member of the Third Division in 1920, QPR
were beaten 2–1 by Watford at home in their first game.

READING

Formed: 1871. Turned professional: 1895.
Nickname: The Royals.
Address: Elm Park, Norfolk Road, Reading.
Telephone: 0734 507878.
Manager: Mark McGhee.
Ground capacity: 12,500.
Record attendance: 33,042 v Brentford, FA Cup Fifth Round, 19th February, 1927.
Record victory: 10–2 v Crystal Palace, Third Division (South), 4th September, 1946.
Record defeat: 0–18 v Preston North End, FA Cup First Round, 1893.
Record transfer received: £325,000 from Watford for Trevor Senior, July 1987.
Record transfer paid: £250,000 to Leicester City for Steve Moran, November 1987 & to Huddersfield Town for Craig Maskell, August 1990.
Honours: Third Division Champions: 1985–86.
Third Division (South) Champions: 1925–26.
Fourth Division Champions: 1978–79.
Simod Cup Winners: 1987–88.
Football League record: 1920 original member Third Division; 1921–26 Third Division (South); 1926–31 Second Division; 1931–58 Third Division (South); 1958–71 Third Division; 1971–76 Fourth Division; 1976–77 Third Division; 1977–79 Fourth Division; 1979–83 Third Division; 1983–84 Fourth Division; 1984–86 Third Division; 1986–88 Second Division; 1988– Third Division.
Managers since the War: Ted Drake 1947–52; Jack Smith 1952–55; Harry Johnston 1955–63; Roy Bentley 1963–69; Jack Mansell 1969–71; Charlie Hurley 1972–77; Maurice Evans 1977–84; Ian Branfoot 1984–89; Ian Porterfield 1990–91; Mark McGhee 1991– .
Some former famous players: Ronnie Blackman; Billy McConnell; Steve Death.

Formed in 1871 following a meeting held at the Bridge Street Rooms in the town.

The club amalgamated with Reading Hornets in 1877 and then with Earley FC in 1889.

They joined the Football League as founder members of the Third Division in 1920. Reading won their first League game, 1–0 away at Newport County.

ROCHDALE
Formed and turned professional: 1907.

Nickname: The Dale.
Address: Spotland, Willbutts Lane, Rochdale, OL11 5DA.
Telephone: 0706 44648.
Manager: David Sutton.
Ground capacity: 10,250.
Record attendance: 24,231 v Notts County, FA Cup Second Round, 10th December, 1949.
Record victory: 8-1 v Chesterfield, Third Division (North), 18th December, 1926.
Record defeat: 0-8 v Wrexham, Third Division (North), 28th December, 1929 and v Leyton Orient, Fourth Division, 20th October, 1987 and 1-9 v Tranmere Rovers, Third Division (North), 25th December, 1931.
Record transfer received: £50,000 from Huddersfield Town for Mark Smith, January 1989 and from Stockport County for David Frain, July 1989.
Record transfer paid: £25,000 to Bolton Wanderers for Mark Gavin, October 1987.
Honours: None.
Football League record: 1921 elected to Third Division (North); 1958-59 Third Division; 1959-69 Fourth Division; 1969-74 Third Division; 1974- Fourth Division.
Managers since the War: Ted Goodier 1938-52; Jack Warner 1952-53; Harry Catterick 1953-58; Jack Marshall 1958-60; Tony Collins 1960-68; Bob Stokoe 1967-68; Len Richley 1968-70; Dick Connor 1970-73; Walter Joyce 1973-76; Brian Green 1976-77; Mike Ferguson 1977-78; Doug Collins 1979; Bob Stokoe 1979-80; Peter Madden 1980-83; Jimmy Greenhoff 1983-84; Vic Halom 1984-86; Eddie Gray 1986-88; Danny Bergara 1988-89; Terry Dolan 1989-1990; David Sutton 1991- .
Some former famous players: Albert Whitehurst; Reg Jenkins; Graham Smith.

Several attempts were made to form a football club in this Rugby League stronghold, before Rochdale Town came into existence in 1900.

When they folded in 1907 a new club was immediately formed and elected to the Manchester League.

A year later the club joined the more powerful Lancashire Combination before graduating to the Third Division (North) in 1921.

Rochdale won their first League game 6–3 against Accrington Stanley.

ROTHERHAM UNITED

Formed: 1884. Turned professional: 1905.
Nickname: The Merry Millers.
Address: Millmoor Ground, Rotherham.
Telephone: 0709 562434. ClubCall: 0898 121637.
Manager: Billy McEwan.
Ground capacity: 15,736.
Record attendance: 25,000 v Sheffield Wednesday, Second Division, 26th January, 1952 and v Sheffield United, Second Division, 13th December, 1952.
Record victory: 8–0 v Oldham Athletic, Third Division (North), 26th May, 1947.
Record defeat: 1–11 v Bradford City, Third Division (North), 25th August, 1928.
Record transfer received: £180,000 from Everton for Bobby Mimms, May 1985.
Record transfer paid: £100,000 to Cardiff City for Ronnie Moore, August 1980.
Honours: *Third Division Champions*: 1980–81.
Third Division (North) Champions: 1950–51.
Fourth Division Champions: 1988–89.
Football League record: 1893 Rotherham Town elected to Second Division; 1896 failed re-election; 1919 Rotherham County elected to Second Division; 1923–51 Third Division (North); 1951–68 Second Division; 1968–73 Third Division; 1973–75 Fourth Division; 1975–81 Third Division; 1981–83 Second Division; 1983–88 Third Division; 1988–89 Fourth Division; 1989–91 Third Division; 1991– Fourth Division.
Managers since the War: Reg Freeman 1934–52; Andy Smailes 1952–58; Tom Johnston 1958–62; Danny Williams 1962–65; Jack Mansell 1965–67; Tommy Docherty 1967–68; Jimmy McAnearney 1968–73; Jimmy McGuigan 1973–79; Ian Porterfield 1979–81; Emlyn Hughes 1981–83; George Kerr 1983–85; Norman Hunter 1985–87; Dave Cusack 1987–88; Billy McEwan 1988– .
Some former famous players: Wally Ardron; Gladstone Guest; Harry Millership; Danny Williams.

The club was formed as Thornhill United in 1884. They

changed their name to Rotherham County in 1905 and moved to Millmoor.

County's first game as a Football League club was in August 1919 when they defeated Nottingham Forest 2–0 at home.

Meanwhile, another club called Rotherham Town had been in existence since 1860 and were playing in the Football League as early as 1893.

Town's first game in the Second Division took place in September 1893 when they drew 1–1 away at Lincoln City.

In 1925 Town amalgamated with County to form Rotherham United.

SCARBOROUGH

Formed: 1879. Turned professional: 1926.

Nickname: The Boro.

Address: The McCain Stadium, Seamer Road, Scarborough, YO12 4HF.

Telephone: 0723 375094. ClubCall: 0898 121650.

Manager: Ray McHale.

Ground capacity: 7,600.

Record attendance: 11,130 v Luton Town, FA Cup Third Round, 8th January, 1938.

Record victory: 6–0 v Rhyl Athletic, FA Cup First Round, 29th November, 1930.

Record defeat: 1–16 v Southbank, Northern League, 15th November, 1919.

Record transfer received: £175,000 from Middlesbrough for Martin Russell, March 1990.

Record transfer paid: £102,000 to Leicester City for Martin Russell, March 1989.

Honours: None.

Football League record: 1987 promoted to Fourth Division.

Managers since the War: Harold Taylor 1947–48; Frank Taylor 1948–50; A.C. Bell 1950–53; Reg Halton 1953–54; Charles Robson 1954–57; George Higgins 1957–58; Andy Smailes 1959–61; Eddie Brown 1961–64; Albert Franks 1964–65; Stuart Myers 1965–66; Graham Shaw 1968–69; Colin Appleton 1969–73; Ken Houghton 1974–75; Colin Appleton 1975–81; Jimmy McAnearney 1981–82; John Cottam 1982–84; Harry Dunn 1984–86; Neil Warnock 1986–88; Colin Morris 1989; Ray McHale 1989– .

Some former famous players: Ray McHale; Colin Morris.

Although they did not achieve Football League status until 1987, at the expense of Lincoln City, Scarborough's history dates back over 100 years.

The club was formed in 1879 by members of the Scarborough Cricket Club.

Their first game in the Fourth Division ended in a 2–2 home draw against Wolverhampton Wanderers and attracted a club record Football League crowd of 7,314.

SCUNTHORPE UNITED
Formed: 1899. Turned professional: 1912.
Nickname: The Iron.
Address: Glanford Park, Scunthorpe, South Humberside.
Telephone: 0724 848077. ClubCall: 0898 121652.
Manager: Bill Green.
Ground capacity: 10,300.
Record attendance: At the Old Showground 23,935 v Portsmouth, FA Cup Fourth Round, 30th January, 1954. At Glanford Park, 8,775 v Rotherham United, Fourth Division, 1st May, 1989.
Record victory: 9–0 v Boston United, FA Cup First Round, 21st November, 1953.
Record defeat: 0–8 v Carlisle United, Third Division (North), 25th December, 1952.
Record transfer received: £400,000 from Aston Villa for Russell Cox, February 1991.
Record transfer paid: £55,000 to Bristol City for Glenn Humphries, February 1991.
Honours: Third Division (North) Champions: 1957–58.
Football League record: 1950 elected to Third Division (North); 1958–64 Second Division; 1964–68 Third Division; 1968–72 Fourth Division; 1972–73 Third Division; 1973–83 Fourth Division; 1983–84 Third Division; 1984– Fourth Division.
Managers since the War: Bernard Harper 1946–48; Leslie Jones 1950–51; Bill Corkhill 1952–56; Ron Suart 1956–58; Tony McShane 1959; Bill Lambton 1959; Frank Soo 1959–60; Dick Duckworth 1960–64; Fred Goodwin 1964–66; Ron Ashman 1967–73; Ron Bradley 1973–74; Dick Roots 1974–76; Ron Ashman 1976–81; John Duncan

1981–83; Allan Clarke 1983–84; Frank Barlow 1984–87;
Mick Buxton 1987–91; Bill Green 1991– .
Some former famous players: Jack Brownsword; Barrie
Thomas; Steve Cammack.

Formed in 1899 when Brumby Hall FC joined forces with
several other local clubs and played on the Old
Showground.
   In 1910 the club amalgamated with another club and
changed its name to Scunthorpe and Lindsey United.
   They dropped the and Lindsey in 1958, eight years after
being elected to the Third Division (North).
   Scunthorpe's first League game at home to Shrewsbury
Town ended in a disappointing 0–0 draw.

SHEFFIELD UNITED
Formed and turned professional:
1889.
Nickname: The Blades.
Address: Bramall Lane Ground,
Sheffield, S2 4SU.
Telephone: 0742 738955.
Manager: Dave Bassett.
Ground capacity: 35,618 (13,600
seats).
Record attendance: 68,287 v Leeds
United, FA Cup Fifth Round, 15th
February, 1936.
Record victory: 10–0 v Burslem Port
Vale, Second Division, 10th
December, 1892.
Record defeat: 0–13 v Bolton Wanderers, FA Cup Second
Round, 1st February, 1890.
Record transfer received: £400,000 from Leeds United for
Alex Sabella, May 1980.
Record transfer paid: £700,000 to Leeds United for
Vinnie Jones, September 1990.
Honours: *League Champions*: 1897–98.
Second Division Champions: 1952–53.
Fourth Division Champions: 1981–82.
FA Cup Winners: 1899; 1902; 1915; 1925.
Football League record: 1892 elected to Second Division;
1893–1934 First Division; 1934–39 Second Divisio; 1946–49
First Division; 1949–53 Second Division; 1953–56 First
Division; 1956–61 Second Division; 1961–68 First Division;
1968–71 Second Division; 1971–76 First Division; 1976–79
Second Division; 1979–81 Third Division; 1981–82 Fourth

Division; 1982–84 Third Division; 1984–88 Second Division; 1988–89 Third Division; 1989–90 Second Division; 1990– First Division.
Managers since the War: Ted Davison 1932–52; Reg Freeman 1952–55; Joe Mercer 1955–58; Johnny Harris 1959–68; Arthur Rowley 1968–69; Johnny Harris 1969–73; Ken Furphy 1973–75; Jimmy Sirrel 1975–77; Harry Haslam 1978–81; Martin Peters 1981; Ian Porterfield 1981–86; Billy McEwan 1986–88; Dave Bassett 1988– .
Some former famous players: Harry Johnson; Billy Gillespie; Alex Forbes; Jimmy Dunne; Joe Shaw; Alan Hopkinson; Graham Shaw; Mick Jones; Eddie Colquhoun; Tony Currie; Trevor Hockey.

The 1889 FA Cup Semi-Final between Preston North End and West Bromwich Albion, prompted several members of Yorkshire County Cricket Club to form a football club to share their Bramall Lane ground.

The move was so successful that Sheffield United were elected to the Second Division three years later.

Their first Football League game ended in a splendid 4–2 home win against Lincoln City.

County Cricket was still played at Bramall Lane until 1973, when the club's new cantilever stand was built.

The car park is now situated where the cricket pitch once was.

SHEFFIELD WEDNESDAY
Formed: 1867. Turned professional: 1887.
Nickname: The Owls.
Address: Hillsborough, Sheffield. S6 1SW.
Telephone: 0742 343122. ClubCall: 0898 121186.
Manager: Trevor Francis.
Ground capacity: 38,780.
Record attendance: 72,841 v Manchester City, FA Cup Fifth Round, 17th February; 1934.
Record victory: 12–0 v Halliwell, FA Cup First Round, 17th January, 1891.
Record defeat: 0–10 v Aston Villa, First Division, 5th October, 1912.
Record transfer received: £1,700,000 from Real Sociedad for Dalian Atkinson, August 1990.

Record transfer paid: £750,000 to West Bromwich Albion for Carlton Palmer, February, 1989.

Honours: *League Champions*: 1902–03; 1903–04; 1928–29; 1929–30.

Second Division Champions: 1899–1900; 1925–26; 1951–52; 1955–56; 1958–59.

Football League Cup Winners: 1991.

FA Cup Winners: 1896; 1907; 1935.

Football League record: 1892 elected to First Division; 1899–1900 Second Division; 1900–20 First Division; 1920–26 Second Division; 1926–37 First Division; 1937–50 Second Division; 1950–51 First Division; 1951–52 Second Division; 1952–55 First Division; 1955–56 Second Division; 1956–58 First Division; 1958–59 Second Division; 1959–70 First Division; 1970–75 Second Division; 1975–80 Third Division; 1980–84 Second Division; 1984–90 First Division; 1990–91 Second Division; 1991– First Division.

Managers since the War: Eric Taylor 1942–58; Harry Catterick 1958–61; Vic Buckingham 1961–64; Alan Brown 1964–68; Jack Marshall 1968–69; Danny Williams 1969–71; Derek Dooley 1971–73; Steve Burtenshaw 1974–75; Len Ashurst 1975–77; Jack Charlton 1977–83; Howard Wilkinson 1983–88; Peter Eustace 1988–89; Ron Atkinson 1989–91; Trevor Francis, 1991– .

Some former famous players: Andy Wilson; Derek Dooley; Ron Springett; Jackie Sewell; Redfern Froggatt; John Fantham.

Like their Sheffield United neighbours, Wednesday owe their existence to a team of cricketers.

The club was formed in 1867 by members of the Sheffield Wednesday Cricket Club, so-called because the team could only play on their half-day holiday which was every Wednesday.

Their first committee meeting was held at the city's Adelphi Hotel and was attended by a Mr. Charles Stokes, who had been one of the founder members of Sheffield United.

The club were elected to the First Division in 1892. Their first League game ended in a 1–0 home victory against Notts County.

Hillsborough, sadly, was the venue for the FA Cup Semi Final between Liverpool and Nottingham Forest on April 15th 1988 at which 95 Liverpool fans died.

This, the worst disaster in British football, prompted the inquiry by Lord Justice Taylor which will have a major impact on the British game in the future.

SHREWSBURY TOWN
Formed: 1886. Turned professional: 1905.
Nickname: Town or The Shrews.
Address: Gay Meadow, Shrewsbury.
Telephone: 0743 60111. ClubCall: 0898 121194.
Manager: John Bond.
Ground capacity: 15,000.
Record attendance: 18,917 v Walsall, Third Division, 26th April, 1961.
Record victory: 7-0 v Swindon Town, Third Division (South), 6th May, 1955.
Record defeat: 1-8 v Norwich City, Third Division (South), 1952-53 and v Coventry City, Third Division, 22nd October, 1963.
Record transfer received: £385,000 from West Bromwich Albion for Bernard McNally, July 1989.
Record transfer paid: £100,000 to Aldershot for John Dungworth, November 1979.
Honours: *Third Division Champions*: 1978-79.
Welsh Cup Winners: 1891; 1938; 1977; 1979; 1984; 1985.
Football League record: 1950 elected to Third Division (North); 1951-58 Third Division (South); 1958-59 Fourth Division; 1959-74 Third Division; 1974-75 Fourth Division; 1975-79 Third Division; 1979-89 Second Division; 1989- Third Division.
Managers since the War: Leslie Knighton 1945-49; Harry Chapman 1949-50; Sammy Crooks 1950-54; Walter Rowley 1955-57; Harry Potts 1957-58; Johnny Spuhler 1958; Arthur Rowley 1958-68; Harry Gregg 1968-72; Maurice Evans 1972-73; Alan Durban 1974-78; Richie Barker 1978; Graham Turner 1978-84; Chic Bates 1984-87; Ian McNeill 1987-90; Asa Hartford 1990-1991; John Bond 1991- .
Some former famous players: Arthur Rowley; Jimmy McLaughlin; Chic Bates.

The club's origins date back to 1886 when a club of that name played on the Old Racecourse Ground.

They did not move to Gay Meadow until 1910. The ground's name was derived from the Middle Ages when the site was used by the local people for fun and games.

Town were elected to the Third Division (North) in 1950. Their first League game away at Scunthorpe United ended in a 0-0 draw.

SOUTHAMPTON
Formed: 1885. Turned professional: 1894.
Nickname: The Saints.
Address: The Dell, Milton Road, Southampton. SO9 4XX.
Telephone: 0703 220505. ClubCall: 0898 121178.
Manager: Ian Branfoot.
Ground capacity: 21,900.
Record attendance: 31,044 v Manchester United, First Division, 8th October, 1969.
Record victory: 7–1 v Ipswich Town, FA Cup Third Round, 7th January, 1961.
Record defeat: 0–8 v Tottenham Hotspur, Second Division, 28th March, 1936 and v Everton, First Division, 20th November, 1971.
Record transfer received: £1,200,000 from Manchester United for Danny Wallace, September, 1989.
Record transfer paid: £1,000,000 to Swindon Town for Alan McLaughlin, December 1990.
Honours: *Third Division (South) Champions*: 1921–22.
Third Division Champions: 1959–60.
FA Cup Winners: 1975–76.
Football League record: 1920 original member Third Division; 1921 Third Division (South); 1922–53 Second Division; 1953–58 Third Division (South); 1958–60 Third Division; 1960–66 Second Division; 1966–74 First Division; 1974–78 Second Division; 1978– First Division.
Managers since the War: Bill Dodgin Snr 1946–49; Sid Cann 1949–51; George Roughton 1952–55; Ted Bates 1955–73; Lawrie McMenemy 1973–85; Chris Nicholl 1985–91; Ian Branfoot 1991–.
Some former famous players: Derek Reeves; Mike Channon; Terry Paine; John Sydenham; Ron Davies; Dave Watson; Peter Shilton; Alan Ball; Kevin Keegan; Danny Wallace.

Formed by players from Deanery FC, a club that came into existence in 1880.

Most of the team were members of the Young Men's Association of St. Mary's Church and in 1885 they held a meeting and decided to form a new club to be named Southampton St. Mary's.

The club did not join the Football League until 1920. Their first game in the Third Division was away at Gillingham and ended in a 1-1 draw.

SOUTHEND UNITED

Formed and turned professional: 1906.
Nickname: The Shrimpers.
Address: Roots Hall Ground, Victoria Avenue, Southend-on-Sea. SS2 6NQ.
Telephone: 0702 340707.
Manager: David Webb.
Ground capacity: 11,863.
Record attendance: 31,090 v Liverpool, FA Cup Third Round, 10th January, 1979.
Record victory: 10–1 v Golders Green, FA Cup First Round, 24th November, 1934.
Record defeat: 1–9 v Brighton and Hove Albion, Third Division, 27th November, 1965.
Record transfer received: £150,000 from Crystal Palace for Glenn Pennyfather, November 1987 and from Wolverhampton Wanderers for Wayne Westley, June 1989.
Record transfer paid: £111,111 to Blackpool for Derek Spence, December 1979.
Honours: *Fourth Division Champions*: 1980–81.
Football League record: 1920 founder member of Third Division: 1921 Third Division (South); 1958–66 Third Division; 1966–72 Fourth Division; 1972–76 Third Division; 1976–78 Fourth Division; 1978–80 Third Division; 1980–81 Fourth Division; 1981–84 Third Division; 1984–87 Third Division; 1987–89 Third Division; 1989–90 Fourth Division; 1990–91 Third Division; 1991– Second Division.
Managers since the War: Harry Warren 1946–56; Eddie Perry 1956–60; Frank Broome 1960; Ted Fenton 1961–65; Alvan Williams 1965–67; Ernie Shepherd 1967–69; Geoff Hudson 1969–70; Arthur Rowley 1970–76; Dave Smith 1976–83; Peter Morris 1983–84; Bobby Moore 1984–86; Dave Webb 1986–87; Dick Bate 1987; Paul Clark 1987–88; Dave Webb 1988– .
Some former famous players: Jim Shankly; Roy Hollis; Sammy McCrory; George Mackenzie; Sandy Anderson.

The club was founded in 1906 and played their first game as a Southern League side on 1st September that year at Roots Hall, their home ground to this day.

The ground was on the site of an old house of the same name and had previously been used by a local amateur club called Southend Athletic.

United became founder members of the Third Division in 1920. They won their first League game 2–0 away at Brighton and Hove Albion.

STOCKPORT COUNTY

Formed: 1883. Turned professional: 1891.
Nickname: County or Hatters.
Address: Edgeley Park, Hardcastle Road, Stockport, Cheshire. SK3 9DD.
Telephone: 061 480 8888. ClubCall: 0898 121638.
Manager: Danny Bergara.
Ground capacity: 8,520.
Record attendance: 27,833 v Liverpool, FA Cup Fifth Round, 11th February, 1950.
Record victory: 13–0 v Halifax Town, Third Division (North), 6th January, 1934.
Record defeat: 1–8 v Chesterfield, Second Division, 19th April, 1902.
Record transfer received: £250,000 from West Bromwich Albion for Paul Williams, March 1991.
Record transfer paid: £60,000 to Derby County for Kevin Francis, March 1991.
Honours: *Third Division (North) Champions*: 1921–22; 1936–37.
Fourth Division Champions: 1966–67.
Football League record: 1900 elected to Second Division; 1904 failed re-election; 1905–21 Second Division; 1921–22 Third Division (North); 1922–26 Second Division; 1926–37 Third Division (North); 1937–38 Second Division; 1938–58 Third Division (North); 1958–59 Third Division; 1959–67 Fourth Division; 1967–70 Third Division; 1970– Fourth Division; 1991– Third Division.
Managers since the War: Andy Beattie 1949–52; Dick Duckworth 1952–56; Billy Moir 1956–60; Reg Flewin 1960–63; Trevor Porteous 1963–65; Bert Trautmann 1965–66; Eddie Quigley 1965–66; Jimmy Meadows 1966–69; Wally Galbraith 1969–70; Matt Woods 1970–71; Brian Doyle 1972–74; Jimmy Meadows 1974–75; Roy Chapman 1975–76; Eddie Quigley 1976–77; Alan Thompson 1977–78; Mike Summerbee 1978–79; Jimmy McGuigan 1979–82; Eric Webster 1982–85; Colin Murphy 1985; Les Chapman 1985–86; Jimmy Melia 1986; Colin

Murphy 1986–87; Asa Hartford 1987–89; Danny Bergara 1989– .
Some former famous players: Alf Lythgoe; Harry Hardy; Jack Connor; Bob Murray.

The club was formed in 1883 by members of the Wycliffe Congregational Chapel.

Called Heaton Norris Rovers until they changed their name to Stockport County in 1890, ten years before joining the Football League.

County drew their first game in the Second Division, 2–2 away at Leicester Fosse.

STOKE CITY

Formed: 1863. Turned professional: 1885.
Nickname: The Potters
Address: Victoria Ground, Stoke-on-Trent.
Telephone: 0782 413511.
Manager: Lou Macari.
Ground capacity: 35,812.
Record attendance: 51,380 v Arsenal, First Division, 29th March, 1937.
Record victory: 10–3 v West Bromwich Albion, First Division, 4th February, 1937.
Record defeat: 0–10 v Preston North End, First Division, 14th September, 1889.
Record transfer received: £750,000 from Everton for Peter Beagrie, October 1989.
Record transfer paid: £480,000 to Sheffield Wednesday for Ian Cranson, July 1989.
Honours: *Second Division Champions*: 1932–33; 1962–63.
Third Division (North) Champions: 1926–27.
Football League Cup Winners: 1971–72.
Football League record: 1888 founder member of Football League; 1890 failed re-election; 1891 re-elected; relegated 1907 and after one year in the Second Division resigned because of financial difficulties; re-elected to Second Division 1919; 1922–23 First Division; 1923–26 Second Division; 1926–27 Third Division (North); 1927–33 Second Division; 1933–53 First Division; 1953–63 Second Division; 1963–77 First Division; 1977–79 Second Division; 1979–85 First Division; 1985–90 Second

Division; 1990– Third Division.
Managers since the War: Bob McGrory 1935–52; Frank
Taylor 1952–60; Tony Waddington 1960–77; George
Eastham 1977–78; Alan A'Court 1978; Alan Durban
1978–81; Richie Barker 1981–83; Bill Asprey 1984–85; Mick
Mills 1985–89; Alan Ball 1989–1991; Lou Macarai 1991–.
Some former famous players: Freddie Steele; Stanley
Matthews; Gordon Banks; Eric Skeels; Geoff Hurst.

Most soccer historians favour 1868 as the year the club was
formed by apprentices of the North Staffordshire Railway.

They became one of the 12 founder members of the
Football League in 1888. Stoke's first League encounter
was a home game against West Bromwich Albion and they
lost 2–0.

SUNDERLAND
Formed: 1879. Turned professional:
1886.
Nickname: Rokermen.
Address: Roker Park Ground,
Sunderland.
Telephone: 091 5140332. ClubCall:
0898 121140.
Manager: Denis Smith.
Ground capacity: 31,887.
Record attendance: 75,118 v Derby
County, FA Cup Sixth Round
replay, 8th March, 1933.
Record victory: 11–1 v Fairfield, FA
Cup First Round, 2nd February,
1895.
Record defeat: 0–8 v West Ham United, First Division,
19th October, 1968 and v Watford, First Division, 25th
September, 1982.
Record transfer received: £275,000 from Manchester City
for Dennis Tueart, March 1974 and from Everton for Paul
Bracewell, April 1984 and from Manchester United for
Chris Turner, August 1985 and from Sheffield Wednesday
for Mark Proctor, September 1987.
Record transfer paid: £700,000 to Middlesbrough for
Peter Davenport, July 1990.
Honours: *League Champions*: 1891–92; 1892–93;
1894–95; 1901–02; 1912–13; 1935–36.
Second Division Champions: 1975–76.
Third Division Champions: 1987–88.
FA Cup Winners: 1937; 1973.

Football League record: 1890 elected to First Division; 1958–64 Second Division; 1964–70 First Division; 1970–76 Second Division; 1976–77 First Division; 1977–80 Second Division; 1980–85 First Division; 1985–87 Second Division; 1987–88 Third Division; 1988–90 Second Division; 1990–91 First Division; 1991– Second Division.

Managers since the War: Bill Murray 1939–57; Alan Brown 1957–64; George Hardwick 1964–65; Ian McColl 1965–68; Alan Brown 1968–72; Bob Stokoe 1972–76; Jimmy Adamson 1976–78; Ken Knighton 1979–81; Alan Durban 1981–84; Len Ashurst 1984–85; Lawrie McMenemy 1985–87; Denis Smith 1987– .

Some former famous players: Charlie Buchan; Dave Halliday; Len Shackleton; Martin Harvey; Jim Montgomery; Dave Watson; Dennis Tueart.

Formed in 1879 as The Sunderland and District Teachers' Association FC, following a meeting in the Adult's School building in Norfolk Street.

After a few months the club suffered financial problems and were forced to recruit new players from outside the teaching profession.

As a result the club was renamed Sunderland AFC in October 1890. They joined the Football League ten years later.

Sunderland's first game in the First Division was against Burnley at home. They were beaten 3–2.

SWANSEA CITY

Formed and turned professional: 1912.
Nickname: The Swans.
Address: Vetch Field, Swansea. SA1 3SU.
Telephone: 0792 474114. ClubCall: 0898 121639.
Manager: Terry Yorath.
Ground capacity: 16,098.
Record attendance: 32,796 v Arsenal, FA Cup Fourth Round, 17th February, 1968.
Record victory: 12–0 v Sliema Wanderers (Malta), European Cup-Winners' Cup First Round (first leg), 15th September, 1982.
Record defeat: 0–8 v Liverpool, FA Cup Third Round replay, 9th January, 1990.

Record transfer received: £370,000 from Leeds United for Alan Curtis, May 1979.

Record transfer paid: £340,000 to Liverpool for Colin Irwin, August 1981.

Honours: *Third Division (South) Champions*: 1924–25; 1948–49.

Welsh Cup Winners: nine times.

Football League record: 1920 original member Third Division; 1921–25 Third Division (South); 1925–47 Second Division; 1947–49 Third Division (South); 1949–65 Second Division; 1965–67 Third Division; 1967–70 Fourth Division; 1970–73 Third Division; 1973–78 Fourth Division; 1978–79 Third Division; 1979–81 Second Division; 1981–83 First Division; 1983–84 Second Division; 1984–86 Third Division; 1986–88 Fourth Division; 1988– Third Division.

Managers since the War: Bill McCandless 1947–55; Ron Burgess 1955–58; Trevor Morris 1958–65; Glyn Davies 1965–66; Billy Lucas 1967–69; Roy Bentley 1969–72; Harry Gregg 1972–75; Harry Griffiths 1975–77; John Toshack 1978–83 (resigned, re-appointed December 1984); Colin Appleton 1984; John Bond 1984–85; Tommy Hutchison 1985–86; Terry Yorath 1986–89; Ian Evans 1989–90; Terry Yorath 1990– .

Some former famous players: Cyril Pearce; Wilfred Milne; Trevor Ford; Ivor Allchurch; Len Allchurch; Mel Charles; Cliff Jones; Jeremy Charles; Leighton James; John Toshack.

There were several amateur teams playing in South Wales before Swansea Town was formed and moved to Vetch Field in June 1912.

The ground is so-called because it was once a field used for growing vetch, a type of bean used to feed cattle.

Swansea became a founder member of the Third Division in 1920. They were beaten 3–0 at Portsmouth in their first League match.

Town became City in February, 1970.

SWINDON TOWN
Formed: 1881. Turned professional: 1894.
Nickname: The Robins.
Address: County Ground, Swindon, Wiltshire. 2N2 2ED.
Telephone: 0793 642984. ClubCall: 0898 121640.
Manager: Glenn Hoddle.
Ground capacity: 16,153.
Record attendance: 32,000 v Arsenal, FA Cup Fourth Round, 26th February, 1972.
Record victory: 10–1 v Farnham United Breweries, FA Cup First Round replay, 28th November, 1925.
Record defeat: 1–10 v Manchester City, FA Cup Fourth Round replay, 25th Janaury, 1930.
Record transfer received: £1,000,000 from Southampton for Alan McLoughlin, December 1990.
Record transfer paid: £400,000 to Bari for Nestor Lorenzo, December 1990.
Honours: *Fourth Division Champions*: 1985–86.
Football League Cup Winners: 1968–69.
Anglo/Italian Cup Winners: 1970.
Football League record: 1920 original members Third Division; 1921–58 Third Division (South); 1958–63 Third Division; 1963–65 Second Division; 1965–69 Third Division; 1969–74 Second Division; 1974–82 Third Division; 1982–86 Fourth Division; 1986–87 Third Division; 1987– Second Division.
Managers since the War: Louis Page 1945–53; Maurice Lindley 1953–55; Bert Head 1956–65; Danny Williams 1965–69; Fred Ford 1969–71; Dave Mackay 1971–72; Les Allen 1972–74; Danny Williams 1974–78; Bobby Smith 1978–80; John Trollope 1980–83; Ken Beamish 1983–84; Lou Macari 1984–89; Ossie Ardiles 1989–91; Glenn Hoddle 1991– .
Some former famous players: Harry Morris; Rod Thomas; John Trollope; Alan McLoughlin.

Formed in 1881 when two local clubs, Spartans and St. Mark's Young Men's Friendly Society, amalgamated.

They joined the Football League in 1920 when elected as a founder member of the Third Division.

Swindon's first game ended in a sensational 9–1 home victory over Luton Town, a result that is still a club League record.

Interesting to note that their County Ground stadium was used as a prisoner-of-war camp during the Second World War.

TORQUAY UNITED
Formed: 1898. Turned professional: 1921.
Nickname: The Gulls.
Address: Plainmoor Ground, Torquay, Devon, TQ1 3PS.
Telephone: 0803 328666. ClubCall: 0898 121641.
Manager: John Impey.
Ground capacity: 5,539.
Record attendance: 21,908 v Huddersfield Town, FA Cup Fourth Round, 29th January, 1955.
Record victory: 9–0 v Swindon Town, Third Division (South), 8th March, 1952.
Record defeat: 2–10 v Fulham, Third Division (South), 7th September, 1931 and v Luton Town, Third Division (South), 2nd September, 1933.
Record transfer received: £125,000 from Manchester United for Lee Sharpe, May 1988.
Record transfer paid: £25,000 to Exeter City for Vince O'Keefe, March 1980.
Honours: None.
Football League record: 1927 elected to Third Division (South); 1958–60 Fourth Division; 1960–62 Third Division; 1962–66 Fourth Division; 1966–72 Third Division; 1972–91 Fourth Division; 1991– Third Division.
Managers since the War: Jack Butler 1946–47; John McNeil 1947–50; Bob John 1950; Alex Massie 1950–51; Eric Webber 1951–65; Frank O'Farrell 1965–68; Alan Brown 1969–71; Jack Edwards 1971–73; Malcolm Musgrove 1973–76; Mike Green 1977–81; Frank O'Farrell 1981–82; Bruce Rioch 1982–84; Dave Webb 1984–85; John Sims 1985; Stuart Morgan 1985–87; Cyril Knowles 1987–89; Dave Smith 1989–91; John Impey 1991– .
Some former famous players: Sammy Collins; Dennis Lewis.

The club was formed following a meeting between old boys of the Torquay and Torbay Colleges at Tor Abbey Hotel in 1898.

They played in local Leagues before joining the Third Division (South) in 1927.

Torquay drew their first League game, 1-1 at home to Exeter City.

TOTTENHAM HOTSPUR

Formed: 1882. Turned professional: 1895.

Nickname: Spurs.

Address: 748 High Road, Tottenham, London, N17 OAP.

Telephone: 081 808 8080. SpursLine 0898 100500.

Manager: Terry Venables.

Ground capacity: 30,952.

Record attendance: 75,038 v Sunderland, FA Cup Sixth Round, 5th March, 1938.

Record victory: 13-2 v Crewe Alexandra, FA Cup Fourth Round replay, 3rd February, 1960.

Record defeat: 0-7 v Liverpool, First Division, 2nd September, 1978.

Record transfer received: £4,500,000 from Marseille for Chris Waddle, July 1988.

Record transfer paid: £2,000,000 to Newcastle United for Paul Gascoigne, July 1988.

Honours: *League Champions*: 1950-51; 1960-61.

Second Division Champions: 1919-20; 1949-50.

FA Cup Winners: 1901 (as a non League club); 1921; 1961; 1962; 1967; 1981; 1982; 1991.

Football League Cup Winners: 1970-71; 1972-73.

European Cup-Winners' Cup Winners: 1962-63.

UEFA Cup Winners: 1971-72; 1983-84.

Double performed: 1960-61.

Football League record: 1908 elected to Second Division; 1909-15 First Division; 1919-20 Second Division; 1920-28 First Division; 1928-33 Second Division; 1933-35 First Division; 1935-50 Second Division; 1950-77 First Division; 1977-78 Second Division; 1978- First Division.

Managers since the War: Arthur Rowe 1949-55: Jimmy Anderson 1955-58: Bill Nicholson 1958-74: Terry Neill 1974-76: Keith Burkinshaw 1976-84: Peter Shreeves 1984-86: David Pleat 1986-87: Terry Venables 1987- .

Some former famous players: Danny Blanchflower; Dave Mackay; Tony Norman; John White; Jimmy Greaves; Bobby Smith; Cliff Jones; Bill Brown; Alan Gilzean;

Martin Peters; Mike England; Martin Chivers; Pat
Jennings; Ray Clemence; Ossie Ardiles; Steve Perryman;
Glenn Hoddle; Chris Waddle.

Formed by a group of old boys from St. John's
Presbyterian and Tottenham Grammar Schools in 1882
and named the Hotspur FC.

They held their meetings at the local YMCA before
moving to the Red House which still houses the club's
offices in Tottenham High Road.

The club was elected to the Second Division in 1908 and
kicked-off their League career with a 3-0 victory over
Wolverhampton Wanderers at White Hart Lane.

TRANMERE ROVERS
Formed: 1885. Turned professional:
1912.
Nickname: The Rovers.
Address: Prenton Park, Prenton
Road, West Birkenhead, Wirral,
Merseyside, L42 9PN.
Telephone: 051 608 4194. ClubCall:
0898 121646.
Manager: John King.
Ground capacity: 14,200.
Record attendance: 24,424 v Stoke
City, FA Cup Fourth Round, 5th
February, 1972.
Record victory: 9-0 v AP
Leamington, FA Cup First Round, 24th November, 1979.
Record defeat: 1-9 v Tottenham Hotspur, FA Cup Third
Round replay, 14th January, 1953.
Record transfer received: £120,000 from Cardiff City for
Ronnie Moore, February 1979.
Record transfer paid: £125,000 to Manchester City for
Neil McNab, January 1990.
Honours: *Third Division (North) Champions*: 1937-38.
Welsh Cup Winners: 1935.
Football League record: 1921 founder member Third
Division (North); 1938-39 Second Division; 1946-58 Third
Division (North); 1958-61 Third Division; 1961-67 Fourth
Division; 1967-75 Third Division; 1975-76 Fourth
Division; 1976-79 Third Division; 1979-89 Fourth
Division; 1989-91 Second Division; 1991- Second Division.
Managers since the War: Ernie Blackburn 1946-55; Noel
Kelly 1955-57; Peter Farrell 1957-60; Walter Galbraith
1961; Dave Russell 1961-69; Jackie Wright 1969-72; Ron

Yeats 1972-75; John King 1975-80; Bryan Hamilton 1980-85; Frank Worthington 1985-87; Ronnie Moore 1987; John King 1987- .
Some former famous players: Bunny Bell; Albert Gray; Harold Bell; Ian Muir.

Formed as Belmont FC in 1884, they changed their name to Tranmere Rovers a year later.

The club almost went out of existence in 1899 when all the players left to join a rival team.

Rovers not only survived, but continued to thrive as one of the best teams in the West Lancashire and Lancashire Combination Leagues.

They became a founder member of the Third Division (North) in 1921 after resigning from the Central League.

Tranmere's first game as a Football League club was against Crewe Alexandra on 27th August that year. They won 4-1.

WALSALL

Formed and turned professional: 1888.
Nickname: The Saddlers.
Address: Bescot Stadium,Bescot Crescent, Walsall, ES1 4SA.
Telephone: 0922 22791. ClubCall: 0898 121104.
Manager: Kenny Hibbitt.
Ground capacity: 12,000.
Record attendance: (at Fellows Park) 25,453 v Newcastle United, Second Division, 29th August, 1961.
Record victory: 10-0 v Darwen, Second Division, 4th March, 1899.
Record defeat: 0-12 v Small Heath, 17th December, 1892 and v Darwen, 26th December, 1896 both Second Division.
Record transfer received: £600,000 from West Ham United for David Kelly, July 1988.
Record transfer paid: £175,000 to Birmingham City for Alan Buckley, June 1979.
Honours: *Fourth Division Champions*: 1959-60.
Football League record: 1892 elected to Second Division; 1895 failed re-election; 1896-1901 Second Division; 1901 failed re-election; 1921 founder member of Third Division (North); 1927-31 Third Division (South); 1931-36 Third

Division (North); 1936–58 Third Division (South); 1958–60 Fourth Division; 1960–61 Third Division; 1961–63 Second Division; 1963–79 Third Division; 1979–80 Fourth Division; 1980–88 Third Division; 1988–89 Second Division; 1989–90 Third Division; 1990– Fourth Division.

Managers since the War: Harry Hibbs 1944–51; Tony McPhee 1951; Brough Fletcher 1952–53; Major Frank Buckley 1953–55; John Love 1955–57; Billy Moore 1957–64; Alf Wood 1964; Reg Shaw 1964–68; Dick Graham 1968; Ron Lewin 1968–69; Billy Moore 1969–72; John Smith 1972–73; Doug Fraser 1973–77; Dave Mackay 1977–78; Alan Ashman 1978; Frank Sibley 1979; Alan Buckley 1979–86; Neil Martin (joint manager with Alan Buckley) 1981–82; Tommy Coakley 1986–88; John Barnwell 1989–90; Kenny Hibbitt 1990– .

Some former famous players: Gilbert Alsop; Tony Richards; Colin Taylor; Mick Kearns; Colin Harrison; David Kelly.

Formed in 1888 when two clubs Walsall Swifts and Walsall Town joined forces.

They decided to drop the Town Swifts from their name in 1895, three years after being elected to the Second Division.

Walsall lost their first League game, 2–1 away at Darwen.

WATFORD

Formed and turned professional: 1898.
Nickname: The Hornets.
Address: Vicarage Road Stadium, Watford, WD1 8ER.
Telephone: 0923 30933. Hornet Hotline: 0898 700272.
Manager: Steve Perryman.
Ground capacity: 26,996.
Record attendance: 34,099 v Manchester United, FA Cup Fourth Round replay, 3rd February, 1969.
Record victory: 10–1 v Lowestoft Town, FA Cup First Round, 27th November, 1926.
Record defeat: 0–10 v Wolverhampton Wanderers, FA Cup First Round replay, 13th January, 1912.
Record transfer received: £1,000,000 from AC Milan for Luther Blissett, July 1983.

Record transfer paid: £550,000 to AC Milan for Luther Blissett, August 1984.

Honours: *Third Division Champions*: 1968–69.

Fourth Division Champions: 1977–78.

Football League record: 1920 founder member of Third Division; 1921–58 Third Division (South); 1958–60 Fourth Division; 1960–69 Third Division; 1969–72 Second Division; 1972–75 Third Division; 1975–78 Fourth Division; 1978–79 Third Division; 1979–82 Second Division; 1982–88 First Division; 1988– Second Division.

Managers since the War: Jack Bray 1947–48; Eddie Hapgood 1948–50; Ron Gray 1950–51; Haydn Green 1951–52; Len Goulden 1952–55; Johnny Paton 1955–56; Neil McBain 1956–59; Ron Burgess 1959–63; Bill McGarry 1963–64; Ken Furphy 1964–71; George Kirby 1971–73; Mike Keen 1973–77; Graham Taylor 1977–78; Dave Bassett 1987–88; Steve Harrison 1988–90; Colin Lee 1990; Steve Perryman 1990– .

Some former famous players: Tommy Barnett; Cliff Holton; Duncan Welbourne; John Barnes; Luther Blissett.

There are several conflicting versions of the club's origins. One states the present club owes it existence to Watford Rovers formed in 1891.

But probably the most accurate story is that the present club was formed by the amalgamation of West Herts and Watford St. Mary's in 1898.

The club were elected to the newly-formed Third Division in 1920, a year after moving to their present Vicarage Road stadium.

Watford defeated QPR 2–1 at home in their first League match.

But the club did not really hit the high spots until the arrival of pop star Elton John as chairman. Elton's influence and money helped Watford reach the First Division and FA Cup Final.

WEST BROMWICH ALBION
Formed: 1879. Turned professional: 1885.
Nickname: The Throstles, Baggies or Albion.
Address: The Hawthorns, West Bromwich, B71 4LF.
Telephone: 021 525 8888. ClubCall: 0898 121193.
Manager: Bobby Gould.
Ground capacity: 36,159 (10,865 seats).
Record attendance: 64,815 v Arsenal, FA Cup Fifth Round, 6th March, 1937.

Record victory: 12–0 v Darwen, First Division, 4th April, 1892.
Record defeat: 3–10 v Stoke City, First Division, 4th February, 1937.
Record transfer received: £1,500,000 from Manchester United for Bryan Robson, October 1981.
Record transfer paid: £748,000 to Manchester City for Peter Barnes, July 1979.
Honours: *League Champions*: 1919–20.
Second Division Champions: 1901–02; 1910–11.
FA Cup Winners: 1888; 1892; 1931; 1954; 1968.
Football League Cup Winners: 1965–66.
Football League record: 1888 founder member of Football League: 1901–02 Second Division; 1902–04 First Division; 1904–11 Second Division; 1911–27 First Division; 1927–31 Second Division; 1931–38 First Division; 1938–49 Second Division; 1949–73 First Division; 1973–76 Second Division; 1976–78 First Division; 1986–91 Second Division; 1991– Third Division.
Managers since the War: Jack Smith 1948–52; Jesse Carver 1952; Vic Buckingham 1953–59; Gordon Clark 1959–61; Archie Macaulay 1961–63; Jimmy Hagan 1963–67; Alan Ashman 1967–71; Don Howe 1971–75; Johnny Giles 1975–77; Ronnie Allen 1977; Ron Atkinson 1978–81; Ronnie Allen 1981–82; Ron Wylie 1982–84; Johnny Giles 1984–85; Ron Saunders 1986–87; Ron Atkinson 1987–88; Brian Talbot 1988–1991; Bobby Gould 1991– .
Some former famous players: William 'Ginger' Richardson; Stuart Williams; Tony Brown; Jeff Astle; Bryan Robson; Lawrie Cunningham.

Formed in 1879 by a group of workers at the Salter's Spring Factory in West Bromwich.

They originally called themselves the West Bromwich Strollers, changing to Albion two years later.

The club became a founder member of the Football League in 1888 and defeated Stoke City 2–0 in their first game.

WEST HAM UNITED

Formed: 1895. Turned professional: 1900.

Nickname: The Irons or The Hammers.

Address: Boleyn Ground, Green Street, Upton Park, London, E13 9AZ.

Telephone: 081 472 2740. ClubCall: 0898 121165.

Manager: Billy Bonds.

Ground capacity: 27,000.

Record attendance: 42,322 v Tottenham Hotspur, First Division, 17th October, 1970.

Record victory: 10–0 v Bury, League Cup Second Round (second leg), 25th October, 1983.

Record defeat: 2–8 v Blackburn Rovers, First Division, 26th December, 1963.

Record transfer received: £2,000,000 from Everton for Tony Cottee, July 1988.

Record transfer paid: £1,250,000 to Celtic for Frank McAvennie, March 1989.

Honours: *Second Division Champions*: 1957–58; 1980–81.

FA Cup Winners: 1964; 1975; 1980.

European Cup-Winners' Cup Winners: 1964–65.

Football League record: 1919 elected to Second Division; 1923–32 First Division; 1932–58 Second Division; 1958–78 First Division; 1978–81 Second Division; 1981–89 First Division; 1989–91 Second Division; 1991– First Division.

Managers since the War: Charlie Paynter 1932–50; Ted Fenton 1950–61; Ron Greenwood 1961–74; John Lyall 1974–89; Lou Macari 1989–90; Billy Bonds 1990– .

Some former famous players: Vic Watson; John Bond; Geoff Hurst; Martin Peters; Bobby Moore; Trevor Brooking; Phil Parkes; Alan Devonshire.

Formed as Thames Ironworks FC in 1895, by workers of the famous East London shipbuilding company.

The players helped to build HMS Warrior, the first ironclad warship.

Sadly the club hit financial problems in 1900 and went out of business. But they were reformed a month later as West Ham United.

They were elected to the Second Division in 1919 and drew their first game 1–1 at home to Lincoln City.

WIGAN ATHLETIC

Formed and turned professional: 1932.

Nickname: The Latics.

Address: Springfield Park, Wigan, WN6 7BA.

Telephone: 0942 44433. Latics Line: 0898 888636.

Manager: Bryan Hamilton.

Ground capacity: 11,434.

Record attendance: 27,500 v Hereford United, FA Cup Second Round, 12th December, 1953.

Record victory: 6–0 v Carlisle United, FA Cup First Round, 24th November, 1934.

Record defeat: 1–6 v Bristol Rovers, Third Division, 3rd March, 1990.

Record transfer received: £200,000 from Coventry City for Ray Woods, January 1991.

Record transfer paid: £65,000 to Everton for Eamon O'Keefe, January 1982.

Honours: *Freight Rover Trophy Winners*: 1984–85.

Football League record: 1978 elected to Fourth Division; 1982– Third Division.

Managers since the War: Jimmy Milne 1946–47; Bob Pryde 1949–52; Ted Goodier 1952–54; Walter Crook 1954–55; Ron Suart 1955–56; Billy Cooke 1956; Sam Barkas 1957; Trevor Hitchen 1957–58; Malcolm Barrass 1958–59; Jimmy Shirley 1959; Pat Murphy 1959–60; Allenby Chilton 1960; Johnny Ball 1961–63; Allan Brown 1963–66; Alf Craig 1966–67; Harry Leyland 1967–68; Alan Saunders 1968; Ian McNeill 1968–70; Gordon Milne 1970–72; Les Rigby 1972–74; Brian Tiler 1974–76; Ian McNeill 1976–81; Larry Lloyd 1981–83; Harry McNally 1983–85; Bryan Hamilton 1985–86; Ray Mathias 1986–89; Bryan Hamilton 1989– .

Some former famous players: Les Bradd; Peter Houghton; Colin Methven.

Formed in May 1932, a year after Wigan Borough had dropped out of the Football League and gone into liquidation.

The committee members of the new Wigan Athletic raised the £2,250 necessary to buy Springfield Park and made an application to rejoin the Football League.

Wigan were turned down and had to wait another 45 years until 1978 when they replaced Southport in the Fourth Division.

They played Hereford United away in their first League game and drew 0–0.

WIMBLEDON

Formed: 1889. Turned professional: 1964.
Nickname: The Dons.
Address: Selhurst Park, London SE25 6PU.
Telephone: 081 946 6311. ClubCall: 0898 121175.
Manager: Ray Harford.
Ground capacity: 13,806.
Record attendance: 18,000 v HMS Victory, FA Amateur Cup Third Round, 1934–35.
Record victory: 6–0 v Newport County, Third Division, 3rd September, 1983.
Record defeat: 0–8 v Everton, League Cup Second Round, 29th August, 1978.
Record transfer received: £1,600,000 from Chelsea for Dennis Wise, May 1990.
Record transfer paid: £500,000 to Reading for Keith Curle, October 1988.
Honours: Fourth Division Champions: 1982–83.
FA Cup Winners: 1987–88.
Football League record: 1977 elected to Fourth Division; 1979–80 Third Division; 1980–81 Fourth Division; 1981–82 Third Division; 1982–83 Fourth Division; 1983–84 Third Division; 1984–86 Second Division; 1986– First Division.
Managers since 1955: Les Henley 1955–57; Mike Everitt 197–73; Dick Graham 1973–75; Allen Batsford 1974–78; Dario Gradi 1978–81; Dave Bassett 1981–87; Bobby Gould 1987–90; Ray Harford 1990– .
Some former famous players: Dick Guy; Nigel Winterburn; Glyn Hodges; Dennis Wise; Dave Beasant; Andy Thorn; Vinnie Jones.

Formed as Wimbledon Old Centrals in 1889, by a group of old boys from Central School.

For over 70 years the club operated in several of the leading amateur Leagues, including the Isthmian.

They defeated Sutton United at Wembley Stadium to win the Amateur Cup in 1963, a year before turning semi-professional.

The club eventually achieved Football League status in 1977 when they replaced Workington Town.

Wimbledon's drew their first League game 3-3 at home against Halifax Town.

WOLVERHAMPTON WANDERERS

Formed: 1878. Turned professional: 1888.

Nickname: Wolves.

Address: Molineux Grounds, Wolverhampton, WV1 4QR.

Telephone: 0902 712181. ClubCall: 0898 121103.

Manager: Graham Turner.

Ground capacity: 25,000.

Record attendance: 61,315 v Liverpool, FA Cup Fifth Round, 11th February, 1939.

Record victory: 14–0 v Cresswell's Brewery, FA Cup Second Round, 13th November, 1886.

Record defeat: 1–10 v Newton Heath, First Division, 15th October, 1892.

Record transfer received: £1,150,000 from Manchester City for Steve Daley, September 1979.

Record transfer paid: £1,175,000 to Aston Villa for Andy Gray, September 1979.

Honours: *League Champions*: 1953–54; 1957–58; 1958–59.

Second Division Champions: 1931–32; 1976–77.

Third Division (North) Champions: 1923–24.

Third Division Champions: 1988–89.

Fourth Division Champions: 1987–88.

FA Cup Winners: 1893; 1908; 1949; 1960.

Football League Cup Winners: 1973–74; 1979–80.

Sherpa Van Trophy Winners: 1988.

Football League record: 1888 founder member of Football League; 1906–23 Second Division; 1923–24 Third Division (North); 1924–32 Second Division; 1932–65 First Division; 1965–67 Second Division; 1967–76 First

Division; 1976–77 Second Division; 1977–82 First
Division; 1982–83 Second Division; 1983–84 First
Division; 1984–85 Second Division; 1985–86 Third
Division; 1986–88 Fourth Division; 1988–89 Third
Division; 1989– Second Division.
Managers since the War: Ted Vizard 1944–48; Stan Cullis
1948–64; Andy Beattie 1964–65; Ronnie Allen 1966–68;
Bill McGarry 1968–76; Sammy Chung 1976–78; John
Barnwell 1978–81; Ian Greaves 1982; Graham Hawkins
1982–84; Tommy Docherty 1984–85; Bill McGarry 1985;
Sammy Chapman 1985–86; Brian Little 1986; Graham
Turner 1986– .
Some former famous players: Bill Hartill; Dennis
Westcott; Stan Cullis; Billy Wright; Bert Williams; Eddie
Clamp; Peter Broadbent; Ron Flowers; Derek Dougan;
Andy Gray.

Formed in 1879 when players from two leading local clubs
St.Luke's and Goldthorn got together and called
themselves Wolverhampton Wanderers AFC.
    The club became a founder member of the Football
League in 1888 and drew 1–1 at home with Aston Villa in
their opening game.

WREXHAM
Formed: 1873. Turned professional:
1912.
Nickname: The Robins.
Address: Racecourse Ground, Mold
Road, Wrexham, Clwyd, LL11 2AN.
Telephone: 0978 262129. ClubCall:
0898 121642.
Manager: Brian Flynn.
Ground capacity: 20,000 (18,000
covered).
Record attendance: 43,445 v
Manchester United, FA Cup Fourth
Round, 26th January, 1957.
Record victory: 10–1 v Hartlepools
United, Fourth Division, 3rd March, 1962.
Record defeat: 0–9 v Brentford, Third Division, 15th
October, 1963.
Record transfer received: £300,000 from Manchester
United for Mickey Thomas, November 1978 and from
Manchester City for Bobby Shinton, July 1979.
Record transfer paid: £210,000 to Liverpool for Joey
Jones, October 1978.

Honours: *Third Division Champions*: 1977–78.
Welsh Cup Winners: 21 times.
Football League record: 1921 original member Third
Division (North); 1958–60 Third Division; 1960–62 Fourth
Division; 1962–64 Third Division; 1964–70 Fourth
Division; 1970–78 Third Division; 1978–82 Second
Division; 1982–83 Third Division; 1983– Fourth Division.
Managers since the War: Les McDowell 1949–50; Peter
Jackson 1951–54; Cliff Lloyd 1954–57; John Love 1957–59;
Billy Morris 1960–61; Ken Barnes 1961–65; Billy Morris
1965; Jack Rowley 1966–67; Alvan Williams 1967–68;
John Neal 1968–77; Arfon Griffiths 1977–81; Mel Sutton
1981–82; Bobby Roberts 1982–85; Dixie McNeil 1985–89;
Brian Flynn 1989– .
Some former famous players: Tom Bamford; Dai Davies;
Dixie McNeil; Arfon Griffiths.

The oldest club in Wales was formed in 1873 by local
businessmen to play a special game against the Provincial
Insurance Company.

In 1876 they became a founder member of the Welsh FA,
but did not achieve Football League status until the Third
Division (North) was introduced in 1921.

Wrexham's first League game away at Hartlepools
United ended in a 2–0 defeat.

YORK CITY

Formed: 1901: Reformed and
turned professional: 1922.
Nickname: The Minstermen.
Address: Bootham Crescent, York,
YO3 7AQ.
Telephone: 0904 624447. ClubCall:
0898 121643.
Manager: John Bird.
Ground capacity: 14,109.
Record attendance: 28,123 v
Huddersfield Town, FA Cup Sixth
Round, 5th March, 1938.
Record victory: 9–1 v Southport,
Third Division (North), 2nd
February, 1957.
Record defeat: 0–12 v Chester, Third Division (North), 1st
February, 1936.
Record transfer received: £100,000 from Carlisle United
for Gordon Staniforth, October 1979 and from QPR for
John Byrne, October 1985.

Record transfer paid: £50,000 to Aldershot for Dale Banton, November 1984.

Honours: *Fourth Division Champions*: 1983–84.

Football League record: 1929 elected to Third Division (North); 1958–59 Fourth Division; 1959–60 Third Division; 1960–65 Fourth Division; 1965–66 Third Division; 1966–71 Fourth Division; 1971–74 Third Division; 1974–76 Second Division; 1976–77 Third Division; 1977–78 Fourth Division; 1984–88 Third Division; 1988– Fourth Division.

Managers since the War: Tom Mitchell 1936–50; Dick Duckworth 1950–52; Charlie Spencer 1952–53; Jimmy McCormack 1953–54; Sam Bartram 1956–60; Tom Lockie 1960–67; Joe Shaw 1967–68; Tom Johnston 1968–75; Wilf McGuinness 1975–77; Charlie Wright 1977–80; Barry Lyons 1980–81; Denis Smith 1982–87; Bobby Saxton 1987–88; John Bird 1988– .

Some former famous players: Bill Fenton; Arthur Bottom; Peter Scott; Norman Wilkinson; Barry Jackson; John Byrne.

A club named York City played from the early 1900's until the outbreak of the First World War when it was disbanded.

They reformed in 1922 and played at Fulfordgate, a ground situated close to the University.

In 1932, three years after joining the Third Division (North), York decided the ground was too far from the city centre and railway station and so moved to their present Bootham Crescent.

York won their first League game in August 1929, 2–0 away at Wigan Borough.

The B & Q Scottish League

ABERDEEN
Formed: 1903.
Nickname: The Dons.
Address: Pittodrie Stadium, Pittodrie Street, Aberdeen, AB2 1QH.
Telephone: 0224 632328.
Managers: Alex Smith and Jocky Scott.
Ground capacity: 22,568 (all seated).
Record attendance: 45,061 v Heart of Midlothian, Scottish Cup Fourth Round, 13th March, 1954.
Record victory: 13–0 v Peterhead, Scottish Cup, 9th February, 1923.
Record defeat: 0–8 v Celtic, First Division, 30th January, 1965.
Record transfer received: £830,000 from Tottenham Hotspur for Steve Archibald, May 1980.
Record transfer paid: £650,000 to PSV Eindhoven for Hans Gillhaus, November 1989.
Honours: First Division Champions: 1954–55.
Premier Division Champions: 1979–80; 1983–84; 1984–85.
Scottish Cup Winners: 1947; 1970; 1982; 1983; 1986; 1990.
League Cup Winners: 1955–56; 1976–77; 1985–86; 1989–90.
Drybrough Cup Winners: 1971; 1980.
Managers since 1975: Ally MacLeod; Billy McNeill; Alex Ferguson; Ian Porterfield; Alex Smith and Jocky Scott (joint).
Some former famous players: Benny Yorston; Joe Harper; Martin Buchan; Charlie Nicholas; Jim Leighton; Jim Bett; Mark McGhee; Gordon Strachan.

Formed in 1903 by the amalgamation of three local clubs, Orion, Victoria United and Aberdeen amalgamated.

Aberdeen had been playing on a ground owned by a man from the village of Pittodrie, situated North of the town.

The new club's first game at Pittodrie Park was a Northern League fixture against Stenhousemuir. A year later they joined the Second Division.

AIRDRIEONIANS
Formed: 1878.
Nickname: The Diamonds or The Waysiders.
Address: Broomfield Park, Gartlea Road, Airdrie, ML6 9JL.
Telephone: 0236 62067.
Manager: Alex MacDonald.
Ground capacity: 11,830.
Record attendance: 24,000 v Heart of Midlothian, Scottish Cup, 8th March, 1982.
Record victory: 15–1 v Dundee Wanderers, Division Two, 1st December, 1894.
Record defeat: 1–11 v Hibernian, Division One, 24th October, 1959.
Record transfer received: £200,000 from West Ham United for Sandy Clark, May 1982.
Record transfer paid: £175,000 to Clydebank for Owen Coyle, February 1990.
Honours: Division Two Champions: 1902–03; 1954–55; 1973–74.
Scottish Cup Winners: 1924.
Scottish Spring Cup Winners: 1976.
Managers since 1975: I. McMillan; J. Stewart; R. Watson; W. Munro; A. MacLeod; D. Whiteford; G. McQueen; J. Bone; Alex MacDonald.
Some former famous players: Jimmy Crapnell; Paul Jonquin; Hugh Baird.

Known as Excelsior FC when formed in 1878. They changed their name to Airdrieonians three years later.

First game on their present Broomfield Park was against Queens Park in 1892.

The club are proud of their Pavilion which still stands to the west of the ground.

Fulham are the only other British League club to boast such a unique feature.

ALBION ROVERS
Formed: 1882.
Nickname: The Wee Rovers.
Address: Cliftonhill Stadium, Main Street, Coatbridge, ML5 9XX.
Telephone: 0236 322350.
Manager: David Provan.
Ground capacity: 8,780.
Record attendance: 27,381 v Rangers, Scottish Cup Second Round, 8th February, 1936.
Record victory: 12–0 v Airdriehill, Scottish Cup, 3rd September, 1887.
Record defeat: 1–9 v Motherwell, First Division, 2nd January, 1937.
Record transfer received: £40,000 from Motherwell for Bruce Cleland, May 1979.
Record transfer paid: £7,000 to Stirling Albion for Gerry McTeague, September 1989.
Honours: Division Two Champions: 1933–34.
Second Division Champions: 1988–89.
Managers since 1975: G. Caldwell; S. Goodwin; D.Whiteford; W. Wilson; T. Gemmell; D. Provan.
Some former famous players: Jock White; Monty Walls; Bunty Weir; Jim Renwick.

The club began in 1882 and played at Cowheath Park, which is now the car park for a large supermarket.

Rovers moved to their present Cliftonhill Stadium in 1919. A year later they made their one and only Cup Final appearance when they lost 3–2 to Kilmarnock.

ALLOA

Formed: 1883.
Nickname: The Wasps.
Address: Recreation Park, Clackmannan Road, Alloa, FK10 1RR.
Telephone: 0259 722695.
Manager: Hugh McCann.
Ground capacity: 3,100.
Record attendance: 13,000 v Dunfermline Athletic, Scottish Cup Third Round replay, 26th February, 1939.
Record victory: 9–2 v Forfar Athletic, Division Two, 18th March, 1933.
Record defeat: 0–10 v Dundee, Division Two, 18th March, 1933.
Record transfer received: £30,000 from Hamilton Academicals for Martin Nelson, 1988.
Record transfer paid: None.
Honours: *Division Two Champions*: 1921–22.
Managers since 1975: H. Wilson: A. Totten; W. Garner; J. Thomson; D. Sullivan; G. Abel; B. Little; H. McCann.
Some former famous players: Jock Hepburn; William 'Wee' Crilley.

Formed in 1883 when the team played on a local public park. They moved to their present ground in 1895.

Alloa made history in 1922 at the end of their first season in the League when they became the first Scottish club to actually win promotion to Division One.

Previously clubs achieved higher status by election.

ARBROATH

Formed: 1878.
Nickname: The Red Lichties.
Address: Gayfield Park, Arbroath, DD11 1QB.
Telephone: 0241 72157.
Manager: Ian Gibson.
Ground capacity: 10,000.
Record attendance: 13,510 v Rangers, Scottish Cup Third Round, 23rd February, 1952.
Record victory: 36–0 v Bon Accord, Scottish Cup First Round, 12th September, 1885.
Record defeat: 0–8 v Kilmarnock, Division Two, 3rd January, 1949.
Record transfer received: £50,000 from St.Mirren for Mark McWalter, June 1987.
Record transfer paid: £20,000 to Montrose for Douglas Robb, 1981.
Honours: None.
Managers since 1975: A. Henderson; I.J. Stewart; G. Fleming; J. Bone; J. Young; I. Gibson.
Some former famous players: Neg Doig; Dave Easson; Jimmy Jack; Tom Cargill.

Formed in 1878 the club took over Old Gayfield, the site of a seashore rubbish dump, two years later.

Arbroath's great claim to fame is their 36–0 victory over Bon Accord: a British record score that is unlikely ever to be beaten.

They joined the Scottish League in 1921.

AYR UNITED
Formed: 1910.
Nickname: The Honest Men.
Address: Somerset Park, Tryfield Place, Ayr, KA8 9NB.
Telephone: 0292 263435. ClubCall: 0898 121552.
Manager: To be announced.
Ground capacity: 18,500.
Record attendance: 25,225 v Rangers, Division One, 13th September, 1969.
Record victory: 11–1 v Dumbarton, League Cup, 13th August, 1952.
Record defeat: 0–9 v Rangers,

Division One, 1929; v Heart of Midlothian, Division One, 1931 and v Third Lanark, Division Two, 1954.
Record transfer received: £300,000 from Liverpool for Steve Nicol, October 1981.
Record transfer paid: £100,000 to St. Johnstone for Sammy Johnston, 1990.
Honours: *Division Two Champions*: 1911–12; 1912–13; 1927–28; 1936–37; 1958–59; 1965–66.
Second Division Champions: 1987–88.
Managers since 1975: Alex Stuart; Ally MacLeod; Willie McLean; George Caldwell; Ally MacLeod.
Some former famous players: Jim Nisbet; Jimmy Smith; Ian McAllister; Steve Nicol.

Formed in 1910 when two local amateur clubs, Ayr Parkhouse and Ayr amalgamated.

The new club took over Ayr's Somerset Park ground and have played on that site ever since.

BERWICK RANGERS

Formed: 1881.
Nickname: The Borderers.
Address: Shielfield Park, Tweedmouth, Berwick-upon-Tweed, TD15 2EF.
Telephone: 0289 307424.
Manager: Ralph Callachan.
Ground capacity: 10,673.
Record attendance: 13,365 v Rangers, Scottish Cup First Round, 28th January, 1967.
Record victory: 8–1 v Forfar Athletic, Division Two, 25th December, 1965 and v Vale of Leithen, Scottish Cup, December 1966.
Record defeat: 1–9 v Hamilton Academicals, First Division, 9th August, 1980.
Record transfer received: None.
Record transfer paid: None.
Honours: *Second Division Champions*: 1978–79.
Managers since 1975: H. Melrose; G. Haig; D. Smith; F. Connor; J. McSherry; E. Tait; J. Thomson; J. Jeffries; R. Callachan.
Some former famous players: Ken Bowron; Eric Tait.

Formed in 1881, Berwick spent their early years playing against clubs in the Northumberland and Border region.

They joined the Scottish League in 1919 rather than the Football League because of their location close to the border. Playing in the English League would have involved away journeys of many hundreds of miles.

BRECHIN CITY
Formed: 1906.
Nickname: The City.
Address: Glebe Park, Trinity Road, Brechin, Angus, DD9 6BJ.
Telephone: 0356 22856.
Manager: John Ritchie.
Ground capacity: 3,491.
Record attendance: 8,122 v Aberdeen, Scottish Cup Third Round, 3rd February, 1973.
Record victory: 12–1 v Thornhill, Scottish Cup First Round, 28th January, 1926.
Record defeat: 0–10 v

Airdrieonians; Albion Rovers and Cowdenbeath, all in Division Two, 1937–38.
Record transfer received: £46,000 from Falkirk for Ken Eadie, July 1986.
Record transfer paid: £15,000 to Dundee United for Gerry Leslie, March 1981.
Honours: *Second Division Champions*: 1982–83; 1989–90.
C Division Champions: 1953–54.
Managers since 1975: Charlie Dunn; Ian Stewart; Doug Houston; Ian Fleming; John Ritchie.
Some former famous players: W. McIntosh.

Formed in 1906 when two local clubs Hearts and Harps decided to join forces.

Brechin were elected to Division Two in 1929.

With a population of around 7,000 Brechin is the smallest town or city in the UK to have its own League club.

CELTIC
Formed: 1887.
Nickname: The Bhoys.
Address: Celtic Park, 95 Kerrydale Street, Glasgow, G40 3RE.
Telephone: 041 551 8654. ClubCall: 0898 121888.
Manager: Liam Brady.
Ground capacity: 48,734 (9,000 seated).
Record attendance: 92,000 v Rangers, Division One, 1st January, 1938.
Record victory: 11–0 v Dundee, Division One, 26th October, 1895.
Record defeat: 0–8 v Motherwell, Division One, 30th April, 1937.
Record transfer received: £1,400,000 from Chelsea for Paul Elliot, July 1991.
Record transfer paid: £1,000,000 to Hibernian for John Collins, July 1990.
Honours: *Division One Champions*: 1892–93; 1893–94; 1895–96; 1897–98; 1904–05; 1905–06; 1906–07; 1907–08; 1908–09; 1909–10; 1913–14; 1914–15; 1915–16; 1916–17; 1918–19; 1921–22; 1925–26; 1935–36; 1937–38; 1953–54; 1965–66; 1966–67; 1967–68; 1968–69; 1969–70; 1970–71; 1971–72; 1972–73; 1973–74.
Premier Division Champions: 1976–77; 1978–79; 1980–81; 1981–82; 1985–86; 1987–88.
Scottish Cup Winners: 1892; 1899; 1900; 1904; 1907; 1908; 1911; 1912; 1914; 1923; 1925; 1927; 1931; 1933; 1937; 1951; 1954; 1965; 1967; 1969; 1971; 1972; 1974; 1975; 1977; 1980; 1985; 1988; 1989.
League Cup Winners: 1956–57; 1957–58; 1965–66; 1966–67; 1967–68; 1968–69; 1969–70; 1974–75; 1982–83.
European Cup Winners: 1966–67.
Managers since 1975: Jock Stein; Billy McNeill; David Hay; Billy McNeill; Liam Brady.
Some former famous players: James McGrory; Jimmy Delaney; Ronnie Simpson; Bobby Evans; Steve Chalmers; Bobby Auld; Pat Crerand; Tommy Gemmell; Danny McGrain; Billy McNeill; Bobby Collins; John Hughes; David Hay; Bobby Lennox; Jimmy Johnstone; Kenny Dalglish; Roy Aitken; Mo Johnston; Charlie Nicholas; Brian McClair.

The club was formed in 1887 as a charity to help the poorer Catholics who lived in Glasgow's East End slums.

Their first game at Celtic Park took place a year later against Rangers. Few of the 2,000 spectators present could have imagined how powerful the two clubs would eventually become, or the intense rivalry that developed.

Celtic became a founder member of the Scottish League in 1890.

CLYDE
Formed: 1878.
Nickname: The Bully Wee.
Address: Firhill Park, 90 Firhill Road, Glasgow, G20 7AL.
Telephone: 041 221 7669.
Manager: John Clark.
Ground capacity: 11,000.
Record attendance: 52,000 v Rangers, Division One, 21st November, 1908.
Record victory: 11–1 v Cowdenbeath, Division Two, 6th October, 1951.
Record defeat: 0–11 v Dumbarton, Scottish Cup Fourth Round, 22nd November, 1879 and v Rangers, Scottish Cup Fourth Round, 13th November, 1880.
Record transfer received: £95,000 from Chelsea for Pat Nevin, July 1983.
Record transfer paid: £14,000 to Sunderland for Harry Hood, 1966.
Honours: *Division Two Champions*: 1904–05; 1951–52; 1956–57; 1961–62; 1971–73.
Second Division Champions: 1977–78; 1981–82.
Scottish Cup Winners: 1939; 1955; 1958.
Managers since 1975: S. Anderson; C. Brown; J. Clark.
Some former famous players: Tommy Ring; Bill Boyd; Brian Ahern; Pat Nevin.

Formed in 1878 and so named because the club's first ground at Barrowfield Park was situated on the banks of the River Clyde.

They joined the League in 1891, moving to Shawfield seven years later.

Clyde were forced to quit Shawfield in 1986 because the club could not raise the £500,000 needed to bring the ground up to the required standard.

The last game at Shawfield was on 28th April, 1986.

Clyde defeated Alloa 4–2, cheered on by a larger than normal 1,200 crowd.

The club now share Partick Thistle's Firhill Park.

CLYDEBANK
First formed: 1889.
Reformed: 1965.
Nickname: The Bankies.
Address: Kilbowie Park, Arran Place, Clydebank, G81 2PB.
Telephone: 041 952 2887.
Manager: J.S. Steedman.
Ground capacity: 9,900.
Record attendance: 14,900 v Hibernian, Scottish Cup First Round, 10th February, 1965.
Record victory: 8–1 v Arbroath, First Division, 3rd January, 1977.
Record defeat: 1–9 v Gala Fairydean, Scottish Cup Qualifying Round, 15th September, 1965.
Record transfer received: £175,000 from Airdrieonians for Owen Coyle, February 1990.
Record transfer paid: £50,000 to Clyde for Gerry McCabe.
Honours: *Second Division Champions*: 1975–76.
Managers since 1975: William Munro; J.S. Steedman.
Some former famous players: Jim Fallon; Blair Miller; Davie Cooper.

The present club's history dates back to 1899 when Clydebank Juniors were formed.

But the club did not achieve League status until 1966, following a brief, but controversial merger with East Stirling. Both clubs regained their separate identities after taking the matter to court.

In 1977 Clydebank were the surprise team in Scotland when they won promotion to the Premier Division.

The same year the club opened a new stand at New Kilbowie with the money raised from Davie Cooper's transfer to Rangers.

COWDENBEATH
Formed: 1881
Nickname: Cowden.
Address: Central Park, Cowdenbeath. KY4 9EY.
Telephone: 0383 511205.
Manager: John Brownlie.
Ground capacity: 7,250.
Record attendance: 25,586 v Rangers, League Cup Quarter-Final 21st September, 1949.
Record victory: 12–0 v St. Johnstone, Scottish Cup First Round, 21st January, 1928.
Record defeat: 1–11 v Clyde, Second Division, 6th October, 1951.
Record transfer received: £35,000 from Heart of Midlothian for Craig Levein, November 1983.
Record transfer paid: £10,000 to Meadowbank Thistle for Neil Irvine, November 1990.
Honours: *Second Division Champions*: 1913–14; 1914–15.
Managers since 1975: D. McLindon; F. Connors; P. Wilson; A. Rolland; H. Wilson; W. McCulloch; J. Clark; J. Craig; R. Campbell; J. Blackley; J. Brownlie.
Some former famous players: Willie Devlin; Jim Paterson.

Formed in 1881 when three teams of local miners decided to amalgamate. Seven years later moved to North End Park, often known as Colliers Den where whippet racing was popular. Moved to Central Park in 1917 after two Second Division Championship successes.

DUMBARTON
Formed: 1872.
Nickname: The Sons.
Address: Boghead Park, Miller Street, Dumbarton, G82 2JA.
Telephone: 0389 62569.
Manager: Billy Lamont.
Ground capacity: 10,700.
Record attendance: 18,000 v Raith Rovers, Scottish Cup, 2nd March, 1957.
Record victory: 13–1 v Kirkintilloch, Scottish Cup, First Round, 1st September, 1888.
Record defeat: 1–11 v Albion Rovers, Division Two, 30th January, 1926 and v Ayr United, League Cup, 13th August, 1952.
Record transfer received: £125,000 from Everton for Graeme Sharp, March 1982.
Record transfer paid: £40,000 to Stirling Albion for Charlie Gibson, 1989.
Honours: Division One Champions: 1890–91 (shared with Rangers); 1891–92.
Division Two Champions: 1910–11; 1971–72.
Scottish Cup Winners: 1883.
Managers since 1975: A. Wright; D. Wilson; S. Fallon; W. Lamont; D. Wilson; D. Whiteford; A. Totten; M. Clougherty; R. Auld; B. Lamont.
Some former famous players: John Lindsay; James McAulay; Kenny Wilson; Graeme Sharp.

The club was formed in 1872 and played at Broadmeadow before moving to their present Boghead Park seven years later.

As the name suggests, the ground at first was no more than a field of thick mud.

In 1913 the club opened their first main stand. It was only 25 feet long and apart from offices and the dressing rooms had seats for 80 spectators.

Called affectionately 'The Postage Box' or 'Hen House' it was the smallest stand on any League ground in Britain.

The structure was sadly demolished in 1979.

DUNDEE
Formed: 1893.
Nickname: The Dark Blues or The Dee.
Address: Dens Park, Sandeman Street, Dundee, DD3 7JY.
Telephone: 0382 826104. ClubCall: 0898 121649.
Manager: Gordon Wallace.
Ground capacity: 22,381.
Record attendance: 43,024 v Rangers, Scottish Cup, 1953.
Record victory: 10–0 v Alloa, Division Two, 9th March, 1947 and v Dunfermline Athletic, Division Two, 22nd March, 1947.
Record defeat: 0–11 v Celtic, Division One, 26th October, 1895.
Record transfer received: £500,000 from Celtic for Tommy Coyne, March 1989.
Record transfer paid: £150,000 to Chelsea for Colin West, August 1990.
Honours: Division One Champions: 1961–62.
First Division Champions: 1978–79.
Division Two Champions: 1946–47.
Scottish Cup Winners: 1910.
League Cup Winners: 1951–52; 1952–53; 1973–74.
Managers since 1975: David Whyte; Tommy Gemmell; Donald Mackay; Archie Knox; Jocky Scott; Dave Smith; Gordon Wallace.
Some former famous players: Alex Hamilton; Doug Cowie; Dave Halliday; Alan Gilzean; Colin West.

Formed when the Old Boys and East End clubs decided to amalgamate after gaining entry to the League in 1893.

Five years later Dundee moved to play on farmland on Dens Road. But the development of their Dens Park stadium did not really begin until the club purchased the site for £5,000 in 1919.

DUNDEE UNITED
Formed: 1909.
Nickname: The Terrors.
Address: Tannadice Park, Tannadice Street, Dundee, DD3 7JW.
Telephone: 0382 833166.
Manager/Chairman: Jim McLean.
Ground capacity: 22,310.
Record attendance: 28,000 v Barcelona, Fairs Cup, 16th November, 1966.
Record victory: 14-0 v Nithsdale Wanderers, Scottish Cup First Round, 17th January, 1931.
Record defeat: 1-12 v Motherwell, Division Two, 23rd January, 1954.
Record transfer received: £900,000 from Coventry City for Kevin Gallacher, January 1990.
Record transfer paid: £350,000 to Newcastle United for Michael O'Neill, August 1989.
Honours: Premier Division Champions: 1982-83.
Division Two Champions: 1924-25; 1928-29.
League Cup Winners: 1979-80; 1980-81.
Managers since 1975: Jim McLean.
Some former famous players: John Coyle; Peter Mackay; Hamish McAlpine; Eamonn Bannon; Davie Dodds; Paul Sturrock; David Narey; Richard Gough.

Formed in 1909 as Dundee Hibernian, in a bid to attract the city's large Irish population.

A few months later, their Tannadice Park ground was officially opened with a match against Hibernian from Edinburgh.

Dundee Hibs drew 1-1 in front of a 7,000 crowd which included special guests from neighbours Dundee.

The club almost became extinct in 1922 after dropping out of the League. But they were reformed as Dundee United and won re-election a year later.

DUNFERMLINE ATHLETIC
Formed: 1885.
Nickname: The Pars.
Address: East End Park, Halbeath
Road, Dunfermline, KY12 7RB.
Telephone: 0383 724295. ClubCall:
0898 121556.
Manager : Iain Munro

Ground capacity: 19,904.
Record attendance: 27,816 v Celtic,
Division One, 30th April, 1968.
Record victory: 11–2 v
Stenhousemuir, Division Two, 27th
September, 1930.
Record defeat: 0–10 v Dundee, Division Two, 22nd
March, 1947.
Record transfer received: £200,000 from Rangers for Ian
McCall, August 1987.
Record transfer paid: £540,000 to Bordeaux for Istvan
Kozma, September 1989.
Honours: *First Division Champions*: 1988–89.
Division Two Champions: 1925–26.
Second Division Champions: 1985–86.
Scottish Cup Winners: 1961; 1968.
Managers since 1975: G. Miller; H. Melrose; P. Stanton;
T. Forsyth; J. Leishman; I. Munro.
Some former famous players: Andy Wilson; Bobby
Skinner; Bobby Robertson; Charles Dickson.

Formed in 1885 when several members of a local cricket
club decided to switch to football and rented East End
Park from the railway.
   The ground had been developed into one of Scotland's
finest by the time they joined the League in 1912.

EAST FIFE
Formed: 1903.
Nickname: The Fifers.
Address: Bayview Park, Methil, Fife, KY8 3AG.
Telephone: 0333 26323.
Manager: Gavin Murray.
Ground capacity: 5,150.
Record attendance: 22,515 v Raith Rovers, Division One, 2nd January, 1950.
Record victory: 13–2 v Edinburgh City, Division Two, 11th December, 1937.
Record defeat: 0–9 v Heart of Midlothian, Division One, 5th October, 1957.
Record transfer received: £100,000 from Hull City for Paul Hunter, March 1990.
Record transfer paid: £29,000 to Montrose for Ray Charles, 1987.
Honours: *Division Two Champions*: 1947–48.
Second Division Champions: 1983–84.
Scottish Cup Winners: 1938.
League Cup Winners: 1947–48; 1949–50; 1953–54.
Managers since 1975: Frank Christie; Roy Barry; David Clarke; Gavin Murray.
Some former famous players: George Aitken; Jock Wood; Henry Morris; George Dewar; David Clarke.

First formed as East of Fife in 1903 by members of football teams from three neighbouring towns.

The club joined the League in 1920, and in 1938 became the first Second Division team to win the Scottish Cup.

East Fife also have the honour of staging the first floodlit Scottish Cup-tie, when Stenhousemuir were the visitors to Bayview in February 1956.

EAST STIRLINGSHIRE
Formed: 1880.
Nickname: The Shire.
Address: Firs Park, Firs Street,
Falkirk, FK2 7AY.
Telephone: 0324 23583.
Manager: Alan Mackin.
Ground capacity: 6,000.
Record attendance: 11,500 v
Hibernian, Scottish Cup, 10th
February, 1969.
Record victory: 10–1 v
Stenhousemuir, Scottish Cup, First
Round, 1st September, 1888.
Record defeat: 1–12 v Dundee
United, Division Two, 13th April, 1936.
Record transfer received: £35,000 from Chelsea for Jim
Dochery, 1978.
Record transfer paid: None.
Honours: *Division Two Champions*: 1931–32.
Second Division Champions: 1979–80.
Managers since 1975: I. Ure; D. McLinden; W.P. Lamont;
M. Ferguson; W. Little; D. Whiteford; D. Lawson; J.D.
Connell; A. Mackin.
Some former famous players: Malcolm Morrison;
Humphrey Jones; Gordon Simpson.

Formed in 1880 as Bainsford Britannia, they played their
early games at Randyford Park, the home of Stirlingshire
Cricket Club.

The club moved to Merchiston Park a few months later
and remained there until moving to their present Firs Park
in 1921.

FALKIRK
Formed: 1876.
Nickname: The Bairns.
Address: Brockville Park, Hope Street, Falkirk, FK1 5AX.
Telephone: 0324 24121. ClubCall: 0898 121554.
Manager: Jim Jefferies.
Ground capacity: 18,000.
Record attendance: 23,100 v Celtic, Scottish Cup, Third Round, 21st February, 1953.
Record victory: 21–1 v Laurieston, Scottish Cup, Second Round, 23rd March, 1893.
Record defeat: 1–11 v Airdrieonions, Division One, 28th April, 1951.
Record transfer received: £100,000 from St. Mirren for Roddie Manley, 1989.
Record transfer paid: £75,000 to Brentford for Eddie May, February 1991.
Honours: *First Division Champions*: 1990–91.
Division Two Champions: 1935–36; 1969–70; 1974–75.
Second Division Champions: 1979–80.
Scottish Cup Winners: 1913; 1957.
Managers since 1975: J. Prentice; G. Miller; W. Little; J. Hagart; A. Totten; G. Abel; W. Lamont; D. Clarke; J. Duffy; J. Jefferies.
Some former famous players: Evelyn Morrison; Alex Parker.

Formed in 1876, the club did not join the League until 1902.

The club's best years came in the 1920's when they broke the British transfer record, paying West Ham United £5,500 for Syd Puddefoot, who later went on to gain England international honours.

FORFAR ATHLETIC
Formed: 1885.
Nickname: Sky Blues.
Address: Station Park, Carseview Road, Forfar.
Telephone: 0307 63576.
Manager: Bobby Glennie.
Ground capacity: 8,000.
Record attendance: 10,780 v Rangers, Scottish Cup, Second Round, 2nd February, 1970.
Record victory: 14–1 v Lindertis, Scottish Cup, First Round, 1st September, 1988.
Record defeat: 2–12 v King's Park, Division Two, 2nd January, 1930.
Record transfer received: £44,000 from Airdrieonians for Kenny Macdonald, 1988.
Record transfer paid: £30,000 to East Fife for Tom McCafferty, 1989.
Honours: *Second Division Champions*: 1983–84. *C Division Champions*: 1948–49.
Managers since 1975: Jerry Kerr; Archie Knox; Alex Rae; Doug Houston; Henry Hall; Bobby Glennie.
Some former famous players: Dave Kilgour; Alex Brash; John Clark.

Formed in 1885 when the reserve team players of Angus Athletic decided to launch their own club.

Forfar joined the League in 1921 after making considerable improvements to their Station Park ground.

HAMILTON ACADEMICAL
Formed: 1875.
Nickname: The Accies.
Address: Douglas Park, Park Lane, Hamilton, ML3 ODF.
Telephone: 0698 286103.
Manager: Billy McLaren.
Ground capacity: 14,505.
Record attendance: 28,690 v Heart of Midlothian, Scottish Cup, Third Round, 3rd March, 1937.
Record victory: 10–2 v Cowdenbeath, Division One, 15th October, 1932.
Record defeat: 1–11 v Hibernian, Division One, 6th November, 1965.
Record transfer received: £110,000 from Dundee for Willie Jamieson, January 1990.
Record transfer paid: £60,000 to Kilmarnock for Paul Martin, 1988.
Honours: *First Division Champions*: 1985–86; 1987–88. *Second Division Champions*: 1903–04.
Managers since 1975: J. Eric Smith; Dave McParland; John Blackley; Bertie Auld; John Lambie; Jim Dempsey; Billy McLaren.
Some former famous players: David Wilson; Rikki Ferguson; Colin Miller.

The club was launched in 1875 by members of the Hamilton Academy, hence the name.

They moved to their Douglas Park ground in 1885. Gradual improvements were made to the stadium down through the years, but the club were one of the last to install floodlights. These were introduced as late as 1971, a year after the club faced disaster.

Faced with serious financial problems, Hamilton quit the League in August 1970. A few weeks later, however, they regained membership and embarked on an exciting new era highlighted by promotion to the Premier Division in 1986.

HEART OF MIDLOTHIAN

Formed: 1874.

Nickname: The Jam Tarts.

Address: Tynecastle Park, Gorgie Road, Edinburgh, EH11 2NL.

Telephone: 031 337 6132. ClubCall: 0898 121183.

Manager: Joe Jordan.

Ground capacity: 29,000 (9,000 seated).

Record attendance: 53,496 v Rangers, Scottish Cup, Third Round, 13th February, 1932.

Record victory: 18–0 v Vale of Lothian, Edinburgh Shield, 17th September, 1887.

Record defeat: 0–7 v Hibernian, Division One, 1st January, 1973.

Record transfer received: £700,000 from Newcastle United for John Robertson, April 1988.

Record transfer paid: £750,000 to Rangers for Derek Ferguson, July 1990.

Honours: *Division One Champions*: 1894–85; 1896–97; 1957–58; 1959–60.

First Division Champions: 1979–80.

Scottish Cup Winners: 1891; 1896; 1901; 1906; 1956.

League Cup Winners: 1954–55; 1958–59; 1959–60; 1962–63.

Managers since 1975: J. Hagart; W. Ormond; R. Moncur, A. MacDonald and W. Jardine; A. MacDonald; Joe Jordan.

Some former famous players: Barney Battles; Jimmy Wardhaugh; Bobby Walker; Dave Mackay; Jim Cruickshank; Alfie Conn.

Formed in 1874, they took their name from a popular dance club in the city, itself named after the novel by Sir Walter Scott.

The club moved to Tynecastle in 1881 and stayed for five years before crossing the road to their present Tynecastle Park.

In an effort to attract support in the early days, Hearts allowed women in free and charged 3d admission compared with the 6d it cost to watch their Edinburgh neighbours Hibernian.

HIBERNIAN
Formed: 1875.
Nickname: The Hibees.
Address: Easter Road Stadium,
Albion Road, Edinburgh, EH7 5QG.
Telephone: 031 661 2159. ClubCall:
0898 121189.
Manager: Alex Miller.
Ground capacity: 23,353 (seated
5,853).
Record attendance: 65,860 v Heart
of Midlothian, Division One, 2nd
January, 1950.
Record victory: 22–1 v 42nd
Highlanders, 3rd September, 1881.
Record defeat: 0–10 v Rangers, 24th December, 1898.
Record transfer received: £1,000,000 from Celtic for John
Collins, July 1990.
Record transfer paid: £350,000 to Oldham Athletic for
Andy Goram, November 1987.
Honours: *Division One Champions*: 1902–03; 1947–48;
1950–51; 1951–52.
First Division Champions: 1980–81.
Division Two Champions: 1893–94; 1894–95; 1932–33.
Scottish Cup Winners: 1887; 1902.
League Cup Winners: 1972–73.
Managers since 1975: Eddie Turnbull; Willie Ormond;
Bertie Auld; Pat Stanton; John Blackley; Alex Miller.
Some former famous players: Lawrie Reilly; Tommy
Younger; Willie Ormond; Arthur Duncan; Joe Baker;
Gordon Smith; John Blackley; Peter Cormack; Des
Bremner; Steve Archibald; John Collins.

Formed in 1875, a year after their Edinburgh rivals Hearts.
They moved to their present Easter Road stadium in 1892,
four years after almost going out of existence.

In May 1888, they had accepted an invitation to open the
ground of another Irish Catholic based club, Celtic.

The Glasgow club were so impressed with Hibs they
poached their best players.

Fortunately Hibs survived and rebuilt a new team
powerful enough to be accepted into the League in 1893.

KILMARNOCK
Formed: 1869.
Nickname: Killie.
Address: Rugby Park, Kilmarnock, KA1 2DP.
Telephone: 0563 25184. ClubCall: 0898 121557.
Manager: Jim Fleeting.
Ground capacity: 17,528 (4,011 seated).
Record attendance: 34,246 v Rangers, League Cup, August 1963.
Record victory: 13–2 v Saltcoats Victoria, Scottish Cup, Second Round, 12th September, 1896.
Record defeat: 0–8 v Hibernian, Division One, 22nd August, 1925 and v Rangers, Division One, 27th February, 1937.
Record transfer received: £20,000 from Celtic for Davie Provan, 1970.
Record transfer paid: £100,000 to Rotherham for Bobby Williamson, 1990.
Honours: *Division One Champions*: 1964–65.
Division Two Champions: 1897–98; 1898–99.
Scottish Cup Winners: 1920; 1929.
Managers since 1975: W. Fernie; D. Sneddon; J. Clunie; E. Morrison; J. Fleeting.
Some former famous players: Joe Nibloe; W. Culley; Perrie Cunningham; Alan Robertson; Bobby Ferguson.

Formed originally as a cricket and rugby club, Kilmarnock did not start playing football until 1873 when they became a founder member of the Scottish FA.

Their Rugby Park ground was used to store oil and coal during the Second World War after which Italian POW's built the North Terracing.

MEADOWBANK THISTLE
Formed as Meadowbank Thistle: 1974.
Nickname: Thistle or Wee Jags.
Address: Meadowbank Stadium, London Road, Edinburgh, EH7 6AE.
Telephone: 031 661 5351.
Manager: Terry Christie.
Ground capacity: 16,500 all seated.
Record attendance: 4,000 v Albion Rovers, League Cup First Round, 9th September, 1974.
Record victory: 6–0 v Raith Rovers, Second Division, 9th November, 1985.
Record defeat: 0–8 v Hamilton Academical, Division Two, 14th December, 1974.
Record transfer received: £115,000 from St Johnstone for John Inglis, June 1990.
Record transfer paid: £28,000 to Albion Rovers for Victor Kasule, 1987.
Honours: *Second Division Champions*: 1986–87.
Managers since 1975: John Bain; Alec Ness; Willie MacFarlane; Terry Christie.
Some former famous players: None.

Originally formed during the Second War War as the Ferranti Thistle works team.

Reformed in 1974 when they joined the League, the first club to do so since Third Lanark became defunct in 1967.

The club dropped Ferranti from their name when offered the use of the new Meadowbank Stadium for their home base by the Edinburgh District Council. Opened in 1970 to stage the Commonwealth Games, Meadowbank has been a major athletic venue ever since.

In fact, the football club have been forced to switch home games to nearby Tynecastle or Easter Road if their games have clashed with the athletics.

MONTROSE
Formed: 1879.
Nickname: The Gable Endies.
Address: Links Park, Wellington Street, Montrose, DD10 8QD.
Telephone: 0674 73200.
Manager: Ian Stewart.
Ground capacity: 6,500.
Record attendance: 8,963 v Dundee, Scottish Cup Third Round, 17th March, 1973.
Record victory: 12–0 v Vale of Leithen, Scottish Cup Second Round, 4th January, 1975.
Record defeat: 0–13 v Aberdeen, 17th March, 1951.
Record transfer received: £50,000 from Hibernian for Gary Murray, December 1980.
Record transfer paid: None.
Honours: Second Division Champions: 1984–85.
Managers since 1975: A. Stuart; K. Cameron; R. Livingstone; S. Murray; D. D'Arcy' I. Stewart.
Some former famous players: Alexander Keillor; Brian Third.

The club was formed in 1879, moving to their Links Park home in 1885, shortly after amalgamating with Montrose United.

Situated beside the seaside, Montrose have allowed their stadium to be used for a number of other activities, including the grazing of farm animals, women's football, a circus and the Highland Games.

MORTON
Formed: 1874.
Nickname: The Ton.
Address: Cappielow Park, Sinclair Street, Greenock.
Telephone: 0475 23511.
Manager: Allan McGraw.
Ground capacity: 16,000.
Record attendance: 23,500 v Celtic, Division One, 1922.
Record victory: 11–0 v Carfin Shamrock, Scottish Cup First Round, 13th November, 1886.
Record defeat: 1–10 v Port Glasgow Athletic, Division Two, 5th May, 1894 and v St. Bernards, Division Two, 14th October, 1933.
Record transfer received: £350,000 from West Ham United for Neil Orr, December 1981.
Record transfer paid: £35,000 to Heart of Midlothian for Roddy MacDonald, September 1987.
Honours: *First Division Champions*: 1977–78; 1983–84; 1986–87.
Division Two Champions: 1949–50; 1963–64; 1966–67.
Scottish Cup Winners: 1922.
Managers since 1975: Joe Gilroy; Benny Rooney; Alex Miller; Tommy McLean; Willie McLean; Allan McGraw.
Some former famous players: Jimmy Cowan; David Hayes.

The club was founded in 1874 and so named because most of the original players lived in Morton Terrace, Greenock.

They were elected to the League in 1893 by which time the club had taken over their Cappielow Park ground.

MOTHERWELL

Formed: 1886.
Nickname: The 'Well.
Address: Fir Park, Motherwell, ML1 2QN.
Telephone: 0698 61437. ClubCall: 0898 121553.
Manager: Tommy McLean.
Ground capacity: 18,000 (3,500 seated).
Record attendance: 35,632 v Rangers, Scottish Cup Fourth Round replay, 12th March, 1952.
Record victory: 12-1 v Dundee United, Division Two, 23rd January, 1954.
Record defeat: 0-8 v Aberdeen, Premier Division, 26th March, 1979.
Record transfer received: £800,000 from Chelsea for Tommy Boyd, May 1991.
Record transfer paid: £100,000 to Newcastle United for Mike Larnach and to Peterborough United for Nick Cusack, July 1989.
Honours: *Division One Champions*: 1931-32.
First Division Champions: 1981-82; 1984-85.
Division Two Champions: 1953-55.
Scottish Cup Winners: 1952; 1991.
League Cup Winners: 1950-51.
Managers since 1975: Ian St. John; Willie McLean; Rodger Hynd; Ally MacLeod; David Hay; Jock Wallace; Bobby Watson; Tommy McLean.
Some former famous players: Bobby Ferrier; Hugh Ferguson; George Stevenson; Willie McFadyen; Ian St. John; Pat Quinn.

Formed when two local clubs Alpha and Glencairn joined forces in the Spring of 1886.

In 1895, two years after achieving League status, Motherwell took over their Fir Park ground, which was situated in the middle of beautiful parkland.

Celtic were invited to officially open the ground, but were hardly gracious visitors. They crushed the home side 8-1 in front of a 6,000 debutant crowd.

PARTICK THISTLE

Formed: 1876.
Nickname: The Jags.
Address: Firhill Park, 90 Firhill Road, Glasgow, G20 7AL.
Telephone: 041 945 4811.
Manager: John Lambie.
Ground capacity: 11,000.
Record attendance: 49,838 v Rangers, Division One, 18th February, 1922.
Record victory: 16–0 v Royal Albert, Scottish Cup First Round, 17th January, 1931.
Record defeat: 0–10 v Queen's Park, Scottish Cup, 3rd December, 1881.
Record transfer received: £100,000 from Watford for Mo Johnston, November 1983.
Record transfer paid: £90,000 to Dunfermline for Grant Tierney, 1990.
Honours: *First Division Champions*: 1975–76.
Division Two Champions: 1896–97; 1899–1900; 1970–71.
Scottish Cup Winners: 1921.
League Cup Winners: 1971–72.
Managers since 1975: R. Auld; P. Cormack; B. Rooney; R. Auld; D. Johnstone; W. Lamont; S. Clark; J. Lambie.
Some former famous players: Alec Hair; George Cummings; Tommy Ewing; Alex Forsyth; Alan Rough; Mo Johnston.

Formed in 1876, Thistle had a number of home grounds before moving to Firhill in the Glasgow suburb of Maryhill in 1909.

During the early days, when they had no headquarters, the club were forced to play home games on other grounds in the city, including Ibrox.

When the club joined the League in 1896, they were playing at Meadowside, a ground situated near Partick on the banks of the River Clyde.

QUEEN OF THE SOUTH

Formed: 1919.
Nickname: The Doonhamers.
Address: Palmerstone Park, Terregles Street, Dumfries, DG2 9BA.
Telephone: 0387 54853.
Manager: Ally MacLeod.
Ground capacity: 13,000.
Record attendance: 24,500 v Heart of Midlothian, Scottish Cup Third Round, 23rd February, 1952.
Record victory: 11–1 v Stranraer, Scottish Cup First Round, 16th January, 1932.
Record defeat: 2–10 v Dundee, Division One, 1st December, 1962.
Record transfer received: £100,000 from Rangers for Ted McMinn, 1985.
Record transfer paid: None.
Honours: *Division Two Champions*: 1950–51.
Managers since 1975: M. Jackson; G. Herd; A. Busby; R. Clark; M. Jackson; D. Wilson; W. McLaren; F. McGarvey; A. MacLeod.
Some former famous players: Billy Houliston; Jimmy Gray; Allan Ball.

The Dumfries club was formed in 1919, joining Division Two six years later.

Their Palmerstone Park ground remained virtually untouched until the end of the Second World War when improvements were carried out by German POW's.

The club were the first in Scotland to have floodlights erected on pylons. They were switched on in October 1958 for a specially arranged match against Preston North End who were then in the English First Division.

QUEEN'S PARK

Formed: 1867.
Nickname: The Spiders.
Address: Hampden Park, Mount Florida, Glasgow, G42 9BA.
Telephone: 041 632 1275.
Manager/coach: Edward Hunter.
Ground capacity: 74,730 (10,000 seated).
Record attendance: 95,772 v Rangers, Scottish Cup, 18th January, 1930.
Record victory: 16–0 v St. Peters, Scottish Cup First Round, 29th August, 1885.
Record defeat: 0–9 v Motherwell, Division One, 26th April, 1930.
Record transfer received: None.
Record transfer paid: None.
Honours: *Division Two Champions*: 1922–23.
B Division Champions: 1955–56.
Second Division Champions: 1980–81.
Scottish Cup Winners: 1874; 1875; 1876; 1880; 1881; 1882; 1884; 1886; 1890; 1893.
Managers/coaches since 1975: D. McParland; J. Gilroy; E. Hunter.
Some former famous players: Walter Arnott; J. B. McAlpine; William Martin.

Formed in July 1867, they are Scotland's oldest club as well as the only amateur club in the League.

They took their name from the Queen's Park Recreation Ground, the club's first home.

During the early years, Queen's Park players formed the nucleus of Scotland's first international teams.

The club joined the League in 1900, 27 years after taking over Hampden Park.

Before that, however, Queen's Park had dominated the Scottish Cup competition, winning the trophy ten times.

They also twice reached the Final of the English FA Cup, in 1884 and 1885. Both Finals were held in Glasgow and were won by Blackburn Rovers.

RAITH ROVERS

Formed: 1883.
Nickname: Rovers.
Address: Stark's Park, Pratt Street, Kirkcaldy, KY1 1SA.
Telephone: 0592 263514.
Manager: Jimmy Nicholl.
Ground capacity: 9,500 (3,075 seated).
Record attendance: 31,306 v Heart of Midlothian, Scottish Cup Second Round, 7th February, 1953.
Record victory: 10–1 v Coldstream, Scottish Cup Second Round, 13th February, 1954.
Record defeat: 2–11 v Morton, Division Two, 18th March, 1936.
Record transfer received: £85,000 from Luton Town for Andy Harrow, October 1980.
Record transfer paid: £35,000 to Partick Thistle for Willie Gibson, October 1981.
Honours: *Division Two Champions*: 1907–08; 1909–10; 1937–38; 1948–49.
Managers since 1975: R. Paton; A. Matthews; W. McLean; G.Wallace; R. Wilson; F. Connor; J. Nicholl.
Some former famous players: Dave Morris; Norman Haywood; Willie McNaught; Ernie Copland.

The club were formed in 1883 and members decided to adopt the name of the local Laird of Raith.

Rovers experienced one of the earliest recorded form of hooliganism when rival fans invaded the pitch during a Cup-tie in 1887.

Local Councillor and businessman Robert Stark had a unique solution to the problem. Mr.Stark, owner of the land on which the club's present ground was built, let loose a bull he kept tied up in a field close to the ground. The bull soon dispatched the offending troublemakers.

RANGERS
Formed: 1873.
Nickname: The Gers.
Address: Ibrox Stadium, Edmiston Drive, Glasgow, G51 2XD.
Telephone: 041 427 5232.
ClubCall: 0898 33 0898.
Manager: Walter Smith.
Ground capacity: 44,500 (36,500 seated).
Record attendance: 118,567 v Celtic, Division One, 2nd January, 1939.
Record victory: 14–2 v Blairgowrie, Scottish Cup First Round, 20th January, 1934.
Record defeat: 2–10 v Airdrieonians, 1886.
Record transfer received: £750,000 from Hearts for Derek Ferguson, July 1990.
Record transfer paid: £2,000,000 to Sampdoria for Alexei Mikhailichenko, June 1991.
Honours: *Division One Champions*: 1890–91; 1898–99; 1899–1900; 1900–01; 1901–02; 1910–11; 1911–12; 1912–13; 1917–18; 1919–20; 1920–21; 1922–23; 1923–24; 1924–25; 1926–27; 1927–28; 1928–29; 1929–30; 1930–31; 1932–33; 1933–34; 1934–35; 1936–37; 1938–39; 1946–47; 1948–49; 1949–50, 1952–53; 1955–56; 1956–57; 1958–59; 1960–61; 1962–63; 1963–64; 1974–75.
Premier Division Champions: 1975–76; 1977–78; 1986–87; 1988–89; 1989–90; 1990–91.
Scottish Cup Winners: 1894; 1897; 1898; 1903; 1928; 1930; 1932; 1934; 1935; 1936; 1948; 1949; 1950; 1953; 1960; 1962; 1963; 1964; 1966; 1973; 1976; 1978; 1979; 1981; 1990–91.
League Cup Winners: 1946–47; 1948–49; 1960–61; 1961–62; 1963–64; 1964–65; 1970–71; 1975–76; 1977–78; 1978–79; 1981–82; 1983–84; 1984–85; 1986–87; 1987–88; 1988–89.
European Cup-Winners' Cup Winners: 1971–72.
Managers since 1975: Jock Wallace; John Greig; Jock Wallace; Graeme Souness; Walter Smith.
Some former famous players: Bob McPhail; Sam English; George Young; Willie Waddell; John Greig; Jim Baxter; Eric Caldow; Jim Forrest; Willie Henderson; Derek Johnstone; Sandy Jardine; Colin Stein; Davie Cooper.

Formed in 1873, Rangers became a founder member of the League in 1890 and have the proud distinction of never being relegated from the top Division.

The club had two homes at Flesher's Haugh and

Kinning Park before moving to a new ground in the Ibrox district of Glasgow in 1887.

Like their previous grounds, the first Ibrox soon proved too small for their ever growing army of fans.

Rangers moved to Ibrox Park in 1899 and kicked-off with a Division One game against Hearts.

That was in December and Rangers were unbeaten League leaders. The club have been setting the pace and achieving success ever since to establish themselves as one of the world's truly great clubs.

Tragedy struck though on January 2nd 1971 when 66 fans died on a stairway at the end of a match against Celtic. Hearing a roar inside the ground, many fans tried to move back up the stairway causing the accident.

ST. JOHNSTONE

Formed: 1884.
Nickname: Saints.
Address: McDiarmid Park, Crieff Road, Perth, PH1 2SJ.
Telephone: 0738 26961.
Manager: Alex Totten.
Ground capacity: 10,169 (all seated).
Record attendance: (at Muirton Park); 29,972 v Dundee, Scottish Cup Second Round, 10th February, 1952.
Record victory: 8–1 v Partick Thistle, League Cup, 16th August, 1969.
Record defeat: 0–12 v Cowdenbeath, Scottish Cup, 21st January, 1928.
Record transfer received: £400,000 from Sunderland for Ally McCoist, August 1981.
Record transfer paid: £115,000 to Meadowbank Thistle for John Inglis, June 1990.
Honours: *First Division Champions*; 1982-83; 1989-90. *Division Two Champions*: 1923-24; 1959-60; 1962-63.
Managers since 1975: J. Stewart; J. Storrie; A. Stuart; A. Rennie; I. Gibson; A. Totten.
Some former famous players: Sandy McLaren; Jimmy Benson; Drew Rutherford; Jim Pearson; John Brogan.

The club was formed in 1884 by members of the St. Johnstone Cricket Club.

They joined the League in 1911, moving to Muirton Park 13 years later.

After winning promotion to the Premier Division in May 1986, Saints took over a new, all-seater, multi-purpose stadium on the outskirts of Perth, named after the farmer who donated the land.

ST. MIRREN

Formed: 1877.
Nickname: The Buddies.
Address: St. Mirren Park, Love Street, Paisley, PA3 2EJ.
Telephone: 041 889 2558.
Manager: David Hay.
Ground capacity: 25,344.
Record attendance: 47,428 v Celtic, Scottish Cup Fourth Round, 7th March, 1925.
Record victory: 15–0 v Glasgow University, Scottish Cup First Round, 30th January, 1960.
Record defeat: 0–9 v Rangers, Division One, 4th December, 1897.
Record transfer received: £850,000 from Rangers for Ian Ferguson, 1988.
Record transfer paid: £400,000 to Bayer Verdingen for Thomas Stickroth, May 1990.
Honours: *First Division Champions*: 1976–77.
Second Division Champions: 1967–68.
Scottish Cup Winners: 1926; 1959; 1987.
Managers since 1975: Alex Ferguson; Jim Clunie; Rikki MacFarlane; Alex Miller; Alex Smith; Tony Fitzpatrick; David Hay.
Some former famous players: Dunky Walker; Billy Abercromby; Iain Munro; Billy Thompson.

Formed in 1877 by members of the St. Mirren Cricket and Rugby Club.

Became a founder member of the League in 1890, moving to their Love Street ground five years later. Situated next door to a slaughter-house the club for a time allowed animals to graze on their pitch for the princely sum of £5 a year.

STENHOUSEMUIR
Formed: 1884.
Nickname: The Warriors.
Address: Ochilview Park, Gladstone Road, Stenhousemuir, FK5 5QL.
Telephone: 0324 562992.
Manager: Dennis Lawson.
Ground capacity: 4,000.
Record attendance: 12,500 v East Fife, Scottish Cup Fourth Round, 11th March, 1950.
Record victory: 9–2 v Dundee United, Division Two, 19th April, 1937.
Record defeat: 2–11 v Dunfermline Athletic, Division Two, 27th September, 1930.
Record transfer received: £25,000 from Rangers for Lindsay Hamilton.
Record transfer paid: None.
Honours: None.
Managers since 1975: H. Glasgow; J. Black; A. Rose; W. Henderson; A. Rennie; J. Meakin; Dennis Lawson.
Some former famous players: Evelyn Morrison; Robert Murray; T. Mullen.

Formed in 1884 as the local village team that played at The Tryst, now a golf course on the outskirts of Falkirk.

The club moved to Ochilview in 1890, but the development of the ground did not really begin until they joined the League in 1921.

STIRLING ALBION

Formed: 1945.
Nickname: The Binos.
Address: Annfield Park, St. Ninians Road, Stirling, FK8 2HE.
Telephone: 0786 50399.
Manager: John Brogan.
Ground capacity: 12,000.
Record attendance: 26,400 v Celtic, Scottish Cup Fourth Round, 14th March, 1959.
Record victory: 20–0 v Selkirk, Scottish Cup, First Round, 8th December, 1984.
Record defeat: 0–9 v Dundee United, Division One, 30th December, 1 967.
Record transfer received: £70,000 from Doncaster Rovers for John Philliben, March 1984.
Record transfer paid: £17,000 to Airdrieonians for Douglas Lawrie, December 1989.
Honours: *Division Two Champions*: 1952–53; 1957–58; 1960–61; 1964–65; 1990–91.
Second Division Champions: 1976–77.
Managers since 1975: A. Smith; G. Peebles; J. Fleeting; J.Brogan.
Some former famous players: Joe Hughes; Billy Steele; Matt McPhee.

Founded in 1945, by a consortium of local businessmen following the demise of another Stirling club, King's Park.

They took over a field on the Annfield Estate and used the adjoining mansion as club offices and dressing rooms.

As there were no stands during the early days, spectators and officials sat on the backs of Albion lorries, hence the name.

The club joined the League in 1947.

STRANRAER
Formed: 1870.
Nickname: The Blues.
Address: Stair Park, London Road, Stranraer, DG9 8BS.
Telephone: 0776 3271.
Manager: Alex McAnespie.
Ground capacity: 4,000.
Record attendance: 6,500 v Rangers, Scottish Cup First Round, 24th January, 1948.
Record victory: 7–0 v Brechin City, Division Two, 6th February, 1965.
Record defeat: 1–11 v Queen of the South, Scottish Cup First Round, 16th January, 1932.
Record transfer received: None.
Record transfer paid: £15,000 to Kilmarnock for Colin Harkness, August 1989.
Honours: None.
Managers since 1975: J. Hughes; N. Hood; G. Hamilton; D. Sneddon; J. Clark; R. Clark; A. McAnespie.
Some former famous players: Dan McDonald; Derek Frye.

The club was formed in 1870, but did not take over their Stair Park ground until 1932.

Gates gradually rose from a few hundred to over the 3,000 that welcomed entry into Division Two in 1966.

Stranraer were the last League club in Britain to install floodlights. These were switched on for a League Cup-tie against Albion Rovers in August 1981.

Index